GOLIATH KILLING PRAYERS

*How To Overcome Every
Spiritual Giant Of Your Life*

LEKE SANUSI

PUBLISHED BY ORAWORD PUBLISHERS UK LTD

First published in the United Kingdom in 2003:

Copyright © 2004 by Leke Sanusi

The moral right of the author has been asserted.

Unless otherwise stated all scriptures have been quoted from the King James Version of the Bible.

All rights reserved.

ISBN 0-95365-340-4

Production: Chosen Graphics 0870 2250041

Illustrations: Chosen Arts

No part of this publication may be reproduced, stored in a retrieval system, or transmitted, in any form or by any means, without the prior permission in writing of the author, nor be otherwise circulated in any form of binding or cover other than that in which it is published and without a similar condition including this condition being imposed on the subsequent purchaser.

DEDICATION

This book is dedicated to my darling wife, Bola, who inspired, encouraged and motivated the writing of this book and to our two children Tobi and Tomi, who are testimonies of Goliath Killing Prayers. To God be all the Glory!

And to all who are under the snare of "Goliath" whom I believe by reading this book will be strengthened and encouraged to fight a good fight of faith knowing fully well that victory is assured in the mighty name of Jesus and that Goliath is just a 'stone throw' to his grave.

ENDORSEMENTS

"Goliath Killing Prayers" has changed my prayer life and added to my spiritual growth and upliftment. Those who desire victory in this endless battle of the end time cannot but avail themselves the prescription to obtaining same as clearly recommended by Pastor Leke in GKPs.

PASTOR DEBO AKANDE
Pastor, The Redeemed Christian Church of God.

Pastor Leke is undeniably an end-time leader in the teaching of prayer. He powerfully articulates his depth of understanding and anointing on the subject of breaking through our battles through fervent prayer. GKPs is an exceptional blueprint handbook that will take your prayer life to a whole new dimension.

KATRINA PRENTICE
Author/Speaker/Evangelist

Having had the privilege of a preview of Pastor Leke Sanusi's GKPs, it is my impression that it is a modest piece of intellectual work inspired by the Holy Spirit to provide a guiding light - a prayer Road Map to all children of the Most High God who are under the yoke and oppression of spiritual Goliaths to have victory in the only name that is above all names, JESUS

HON. JUSTICE G.O. KOLAWOLE
Judge, Federal High Court

Table Of Content

FOREWORD — V
ACKNOWLEGEMENT — IV
PREFACE — VI

PART ONE
WHO IS GOLIATH?.....................................1
(Understanding The Giant of Your Life)
1. GOLIATH IS A STUBBORN PROBLEM............9
2. GOLIATH IS NOT OF THIS WORLD.............16
3. GOLIATH INSTILLS FEAR..........................24
4. GOLIATH IS A REPROACH.........................39
5. GOLIATH IS A GIANT OBSTACLE................51

PART TWO
WHAT IS GOLIATH KILLING PRAYERS (GKP)..62
(Understanding The Giant of Your Life)
6. GKP IS BOLD....................................66
7. GKP IS PERSISTENT............................78
8. GKP IS POWERFUL AND AUTHORITATIVE   90
9. GKP IS FULL OF FAITH.........................102
10. GKP IS OFFENSIVE.............................112
11. GKP IS PREVAILING............................120
12. "WHOSE SON ART THOU ?"....................128

FOREWORD

Goliath Killing Prayers is the long awaited sequel to Pastor Leke Sanusi's international best-seller " None Shall be Barren."

In this well written book, Pastor Leke shed much light on Goliath and what he represents in this end time.

Many Christians who are destined to be giant killers are not maximizing their potentials and fulfilling their destinies because of the problems of ignorance and fear.

Goliath operates through fear. Thus, Pastor Leke seriously dealt with the issue of fear, which is the greatest tormentor of mankind today. Goliath threatened Israel for forty days but it took David less than five minutes to destroy him. Pastor Leke thus, avers that just as every Goliath has an unguarded forehead, every problem has a solution - the five smooth stones, JESUS.

In a lucid manner, the author used case studies to elucidate that fear and faith do not mix and that we need boldness, persistence and authority to activate prevailing faith. He strongly recommends that our prayers should be offensive not defensive.

Pastor Leke whose ministry of prevailing prayers comes to the fore in this book also recommended some prayer arrows that will destroy any giant, obstacle, problem or limitations that may want to stop you from getting to your throne.

In this era of anxiety and fear of all sorts, this book is a must read for all those who are in desperate need of antidotes to their seemingly intractable problems.

You must read this book!

PASTOR BROWN OYITSO
Provincial Pastor
The Redeemed Christian Church Of God

ACKNOWLEDGMENT

My gratitude to God Almighty who took me out of the miry clay and set my feet upon the Rock. You will forever be my Lord and God.

I am indebted to many, too numerous to mention who have impacted my life and made it possible for me to tread on the path of my God-given destiny. Space does not permit me to mention them all, but I must acknowledge the direct contributions of some to the success of this book. I am grateful to Katrina Prentice who gave the manuscript a thorough read and made thoughtful suggestions. I thank Pastor Debo Akande and Hon. Justice G.O. Kolawole for reading the manuscripts and giving encouraging words. I want to thank you all at Chosengraphics for quenching all the fiery darts of 'Goliath' who tried hard to stop the publication of this book, but failed.

My appreciation goes to Pastor Brown Oyitso, for writing the Forword to this book in spite of the extremely short notice he had. He is a father-in- the Lord indeed! I am eternally grateful to Pastor Enoch Adeboye, General Overseer of the Redeemed Christian Church of God. He prayed the one prayer that took every anti-destiny Goliath out of my way, that prayer was *"Lord, scatter them abroad."*

I thank all members of RCCG Victory House, London. It is a great privilege to be God's servant to you. To my darling wife, Bola, for being my "Help meet" indeed, thank you and my two miracle boys, Tobi and Tomi, thank you, for being God's gifts to me.

Leke Sanusi
London
May 2003

PREFACE

GOLIATH still exists. Although he was slain by David several thousands of years ago, his spirit lives on. Someone said, "Goliath has children." I tend to agree. The children of Goliath are the spirits he represents today and those spirits are the giants standing tall against you, desperate to deny you from the fulfilment of your God-given destiny.

God had great plans and purposes for you when He created you. You were well thought of long before you came into this world.

> *"For I know the thoughts that I think toward you, saith the Lord, thoughts of peace and not of evil, to give you an expected end." (Jer.29:11)*

Even so, you are not to sit back and expect that your expected end, as planned by God, will just begin to come to pass without you having to do anything. It doesn't work that way. The next two verses say,

> *"Then shall ye call upon me, and ye shall go and pray unto me, and I will hearken unto you. And ye shall seek me and find me, when ye shall search for me, with all your heart ".(verses 12&13).*

There are some operative words in those two verses: *"shall"*, *"call"*, *"go"*, *"pray"*, *"seek"*, *"find"* *"search"*.

These words, and the context in which they appear, led me to one inevitable conclusion, in order for you to realise and live God's plan and purpose for your life, you have a war to fight. The war is not a physical one but spiritual. No wonder *Ephesians 6:12* says,

"For we wrestle not against flesh and blood, but against principalities, against powers, against the rulers of the darkness of this world, against spiritual wickedness in high places."

I spent time studying the story of David and Goliath *(1Sam. 17:1-58)* and concluded that the story has not ended. It continues and right now it is continuing in your life. There is a throne prepared for you, but there is a Goliath standing in your way to it, AND if you do not kill that Goliath, you cannot ascend the throne destined for you. The journey to the palace of your destiny climaxes not in the parlour of your family house, but in the battlefield of life where Goliath stands tall to resist you.

I decided to write this book in order to expose your Goliath and give you some powerful keys for unlocking his hidden identity as he continues to operate through his 'children' today. When you read this book, you will be able to recognize the particular giant that stands in the path to your throne. Then you will understand the practical principles of prayer that you need to apply in order to overcome your Goliath. Just as the weapon of David against Goliath was peculiar, your weapon for overcoming your Goliath must be peculiar and unique, certainly not carnal. *"For the weapons of our warfare are not carnal,*

Goliath. Just as the weapon of David against Goliath was peculiar, your weapon for overcoming your Goliath must be peculiar and unique, certainly not carnal.

"For the weapons of our warfare are not carnal, but mighty through God to the pulling down of strongholds. "(IICor.10:4)

You must be ready to 'fight the good fight of faith'. You have a responsibility and a duty to bring God's plan and purpose for your life to pass. You must rescue and recover every department of your life (health, career, marriage, finance, family, future etc) from the control and domination of Goliath.

Part One of this book will help you to expose your Goliath, whilst Part Two will help you to exterminate him. My strong advice to you is, as you go through the book, you must not proceed to the next chapter without forcefully praying the prayer points at the end of the preceding chapter. Remember,

> *"And from the days of John the Baptist until now the Kingdom of heaven suffereth violence, and the violent take it by force." (Matt. 11:12).*

Therefore, get spiritually violent!

As you read and aggressively pray and take action, I pray that God will anoint you afresh with power and the Holy Ghost to overcome every Goliath in your life and ascend the Throne of your Destiny in the mighty name of Jesus. I look forward to reading your testimonies and being part of your thanksgiving to God Almighty who alone is Worthy to be Praised!

PART

WHO IS GOLIATH?
Understanding the Giant of Your Life

Understanding the root of any problem is pivotal to finding a solution to it. Proper and adequate knowledge produce understanding. Knowledge acted upon produces power and power properly applied produces desired results.

The Bible says some people had understanding of the times and as a result they knew what a whole nation ought to do. We read this in 1Chro. 12:32

> *"And of the children of Issachar, which were men that had understanding of the times, to know what Israel ought to do…"*

May God give us men like that as leaders in our nations and make you, the reader one of such men. When you have understanding, you defeat ignorance which is a deadly disease.

"My people are destroyed for lack of knowledge..." (Hosea 4:6)

Understanding makes you outstanding. When you know who the Goliath of your life is, you will no longer wonder *why* you are going through what you are going through. Then you will be prepared to assimilate the practical principles for dealing with Goliath, gaining victory over him and liberating yourself from his oppression.

In this book, the story of David and Goliath in the Bible is the foundation for understanding and dealing with Goliath in our lives. I quote copiously from *1Samuel 17:26-52* (Please do not skip, be sure to read the entire scripture for a better understanding of this book):

> *"And David spake to the men that stood by him, saying, what shall be done to the man that killeth this Philistine, and taketh away the reproach from Israel? For who is this uncircumcised Philistine, that he should defy the armies of the living God?*
>
> *And the people answered him after this manner, saying, so shall it be done to the man that killeth him.*
>
> *And Eliab his eldest brother heard when he spake unto the men; and Eliab's anger was kindled against David, and he said, why camest thou down hither? And with whom hast thou left those few sheep in the wilderness? I know thy pride, and the naughtiness of thine heart; for*

WHO IS GOLIATH?

thou hath come down that thou mightest see the battle.

And David said, what have I now done? Is there not a cause?

And he returned from him toward another, and spake after the same manner: and the people answered him again after the former manner.

And when the words were heard which David spake, they rehearsed them before Saul: and he sent for him.

And David said to Saul, Let no man's heart fail because of him; thy servant will go and fight with this Philistine.

And Saul said to David, Thou art not able to go against this Philistine to fight with him: for thou art but a youth, and he a man of war from his youth.

And David said unto Saul, Thy servant kept his fathers's sheep, and there came a lion, and a bear, and took a lamb out of the flock:

And I went out after him and smote him, and delivered it out of his mouth: and when he arose against me, I caught him by his beard, and smote him and slew him.

Thy servant slew both the lion and the bear: and this uncircumcised Philistine shall be as one of them, seeing he hath defied the armies of the living God.

David said moreover, the Lord that delivered me out of the paw of the lion, and out of the paw of the bear, he will deliver me out of the hand of this Philistine. And Saul said unto David, Go, and the Lord be with thee.

And Saul armed David with his armour, and he put an helmet of brass upon his head; also he armed him with a coat of mail.

And David girded his sword upon his armour, and he assayed to go; for he had not proved it. And David said unto Saul, I cannot go with these; for I have not proved them. And David put them off him.

And he took his staff in his hand, and chose him five smooth stones out of the brook, and put them in a shepherd's bag which he had, even in a scrip; and his sling was in his hand: and he drew near to the Philistine.

And the Philistine came on and drew near unto David; and the man that bare the shield went before him.

And when the Philistine looked about, and saw David, he disdained him: for he was but a youth, and ruddy, and of a fair countenance.

And the Philistine said unto David, Am I a dog, that thou comest to me with staves? And the Philistine cursed David by his gods.

And the Philistine said to David, come to me, and I will give thy flesh unto the fowls of the air, and to the beasts of the field.

WHO IS GOLIATH?

Then said David to the Philistine, thou comest to me with a sword, and with a spear, and with a shield: but I come to thee in the name of the Lord of hosts, the God of the armies of Israel, whom thou has defied.

This day will the Lord deliver thee into mine hand and I will smite thee, and take thine head from thee; and I will give the carcases of the host of the Philistine this day unto the fowls of the air, and to the wild beasts of the earth; and that all the earth may know that there is a God in Israel.

And all this assembly shall know that the Lord saveth not with sword and spear: for the battle is the Lord's and he will give you into our hands.

And it came to pass when the Philistine arose, and came and drew nigh to meet David, that David hasted, and ran toward the army to meet the Philistine.

And David put his hand in his bag, and took thence a stone, and slang it, and smote the Philistine in his forehead, that the stone sunk into his forehead; and he fell upon his face to the earth.

So David prevailed over the Philistine with a sling and with a stone, and smote the Philistine, and slew him; but there was no sword in the hand of David.

Therefore, David ran, and stood upon the Philistine, and took his sword, and drew it out of the sheath there-

of, and slew him, and cut off his head therewith. And when the Philistines saw their champion was dead, they fled."

BACKGROUND FACTS

There are some important background facts to the scriptures above that we need to bear in mind. I want to list ten of them in brief:

1. David had just been anointed with oil as future King of Israel, to replace Saul, the incumbent.

2. The Spirit of the Lord, the Holy Ghost, had come upon David.

3. The Philistines came to battle against Israel.

4. Goliath, a ten feet tall champion, led the Philistines.

5. Goliath challenged the Israelites to a one-to-one combat and offered himself.

6. Twice daily, he challenged them for forty days.

7. The Israelites were terribly afraid of the Philistines' champion. Saul, their tallest man and king was no match for him.

8. One day, Jesse, the father of David sent him to meet with his brothers in the battlefield.

9. While there, David saw Goliath tormenting and threatening the Israelites and the latter were fleeing from him.

10. This prompted David to take some decisive action which started with his enquiry in 1Samuel 17:26 quoted above.

Before you proceed to reading the first chapter of this book, I want you to pray the following prayer points aloud:

PRAYER ARROWS

▶ *Father, I confess my spiritual carelessness and scriptural ignorance, forgive me and have mercy upon me in the name of Jesus.*

▶ *Holy Spirit, visit the foundation of ignorance in my life and uproot it in the name of Jesus.*

▶ *Father, reveal to me the truth of any problem of my life in the name of Jesus.*

▶ *Lord, expose the Goliath of my life and prepare me for battle against him in the name of Jesus.*

▶ *Lord Jesus, I surrender my life to you completely.*

▶ *Father, give me understanding and make me outstanding in the name of Jesus.*

- *Holy Ghost, show me clearly the weapon in my hand for slaying my Goliath in the name of Jesus.*

- *Right now I receive divine prescription to every problem in my life in the name of Jesus.*

- *Let my ears be opened to instructions and let my heart be opened to understanding in the name of Jesus.*

- *Lord, make me a weapon of war in the name of Jesus.*

- *Thank you Father for your assurance of victory in the name of Jesus. AMEN.*

Chapter One

GOLIATH IS A STUBBORN PROBLEM

"And the Philistine drew near morning and evening and presented himself forty days." 1Sam. 17:16

Goliath is any stubborn problem that keeps threatening, troubling and tormenting your life. This could be anything from sickness to a particularly trying situation. It could be an opposition or perhaps, a recurring negative pattern. If you study the manner of 'Mr Goliath' in the story, you will understand what we are saying here. Let us look at how Goliath troubled Israel.

"And the Philistine drew near morning and evening, and presented himself forty days". (1Sam. 17:16)

Everyday, Goliath came to the Israelites. He came in

the morning, and in the evening. What was his mission? He threatened the Israelites. He said to them:

> "...choose you a man for you, and let him come down to me. If he be able to fight with me, and kill me, then will we (the Philistines) be your servants: but if I prevail against him, and kill him, then shall ye be our servants, and serve us."(vs.8-9)

For forty days, he continued his unrepentant threat. That is what your Goliath is doing to you right now and you must deal with it. If you have a symptom that threatens your body on a daily basis, not allowing you to rest, you have a Goliath that you must exterminate.

I have been in that situation before. For about forty days I was threatened with a sickness called insomnia. (Inability to sleep naturally and normally). There was absolutely no natural cause I could attribute it to. It was very stubborn and unyielding. It took serious spiritual warfare and combined intercessions of several intercessors to 'kill this Goliath' out of my life.

A young lady once came to me about a persistent problem. She had been bleeding everyday for six months; it was a pathetic case but I was reminded of the woman with the issue of blood in the Bible. This lady had a stubborn Goliath she needed to deal with. We decided to deal with this stubborn problem over three days of prayer with fasting. We prayed together for a considerable length of time every evening for three days. They were violent prayers. That is the language Goliath speaks; he was challenging Israel to a violent confrontation. After three days of battle, we declared victory over this 'Goliath' tormenting the lady. Nothing changed in the physical realm over the next few days and when she came back to me I assured her that her Goliath was dead and that she should stop seeing his 'ghost' (the continued bleeding). Rather, she was to keep thanking and praising God. And that was it; she went away and the issue of blood dried up. She saw this 'Goliath' no more. it was wonderful hearing her give her testimony in Church the following week to the glory of God. In this same way, your Goliath will die in the name of Jesus.

A Goliath also comes in the form of a demonic dream that may keep recurring. I know for a fact that some people do experience this problem. Evil dreams and nightmares that keep coming back and tormenting them. That is a Goliath and they had better do something quickly. Pray 'Goliath Killing Prayers.'

Recently, a member of my church had such a problem. She had been dreaming of death for several days; her late mother kept showing up in her dreams calling her to 'the other side.' Anytime she tried to sleep, day or night (like Goliath), this dream would appear in her mind. According to her, it became so persistently troubling that she became afraid of sleeping. One Sunday, in the course of the church service, we began to pray some serious prayers. The Lord told me that there was someone in the service who was being tormented by evil dreams of death everyday and that He was dealing with this case. Right there and then, I just announced what God had said and we kept praying to slay every Goliath. Unknown to me, the lady going through these experiences was in the congregation. She *claimed* her deliverance and as soon as she got home, she slept like a baby for several UNBROKEN hours. In the night, she phoned me to relate her story. To this day, that evil dream never came back again. **Your 'Goliath' will not come back in the name of Jesus.**

> *"What do you imagine against the Lord? He will make an utter end: affliction shall not rise up the second time." (Nahum 1:9)*

Is there a problem that confronts you in the eyes, stares you in the face, morning and evening, for days, for weeks, months or even years? That problem is a Goliath and the Lord will give you the tongue to pray Goliath Killing Prayers.

Goliath is a 'thorn in the flesh.' Hear what Paul said:

> *"...there was given to me a thorn in the flesh, the messenger of Satan to buffet me, ...For this thing I besought the Lord thrice, that it might depart from me...." (2 Cor. 12:7)*

WHO IS GOLIATH?

You see, that problem did not want to go, it kept tormenting Paul. It took the grace of God for him to overcome. **You will also overcome your Goliath by the grace of God.** One thing you must learn from Paul is that you don't keep quiet about Goliaths (thorn in the flesh). You must call upon God, not once, not twice but *many* times until you receive victory. *"Pray without ceasing."(1 Thes. 5:17)*

It could also be the thought of the problem that is tormenting you day and night. As with the children of Israel, the mere thought of Goliath made them tremble. In fact, I am sure that when they went to bed at night, they even dreamt of Goliath.

Israel carried Goliath twenty-four hours a day. He was a yoke to them. Many of them would have developed stomach ulcers; many of them would have had terrible sicknesses because of the persistent, stubborn and lingering thoughts and threats of Goliath. Are you being confronted with such situation in your life? If so, I challenge you to get ready and step up. There is a Goliath to be destroyed right now!

PRAYER ARROWS

➤ *Lord I thank you for you are my refuge in times of trouble.*

➤ *Lord, behold the threatening of my Goliath and stretch forth your hand against him in the name of Jesus.*

- Father, I give you permission to trouble every trouble of my life in the name of Jesus.

- Let every stubborn problem receive destruction now in the name of Jesus.

- I command every lingering problem to evaporate now in the name of Jesus.

- I refuse to serve Goliath in the name of Jesus.

- Holy Spirit, keep my heart and mind at perfect peace in the name of Jesus.

- I receive deliverance from daily anxieties and nightly worries in the name of Jesus.

- The Goliath I saw today, I will see you no more forever in the name of Jesus.

- Let the fountain of any sickness in my body dry up now in the name of Jesus.

- I set fire upon any satanic messenger tormenting my life in the name of Jesus.

- I shake off every beast called 'Goliath' out of my life in the name of Jesus.

- I saturate my life with the blood of Jesus and I declare that there is no place for Goliath in the name of Jesus.

- Every spirit of Goliath tormenting me in my dreams, melt away right now in the name of Jesus. AMEN.

Chapter Two

GOLIATH IS NOT OF THIS WORLD

> *"And there went out a champion out of the camp of the Philistine named Goliath of Gath whose height was six cubits and a span"* (1 Sam. 17:4)

Who is Goliath? A situation that seems beyond human comprehension or understanding is a Goliath. You look at such a situation and you say, "Where is this coming from?" "I cannot understand this." It is like a case from outer space. You know that something is wrong somewhere but you cannot pinpoint what, where and why. It is simply not of this world.

Friend, what you are wondering about is a Goliath. Read *1Sam. 17:4* again and you will know that Goliath is not of this world.

> *"And a champion went out of the camp of the Philistines named Goliath of Gath, whose height was six cubits and a span (almost ten feet)."*

WHO IS GOLIATH?

That is it! Goliath was almost TEN FEET TALL Have you ever seen a man ten feet tall? I haven't. Even, Saul, the King and the tallest man in Israel was no match for Goliath.

> "...Saul, ...from his shoulders and upward he was higher than any of the people." (1Sam.9 :2)

Therefore, Goliath is not of this world, he is beyond human comprehension. Yes, he existed and confronted Israel. But what I am saying now is that Goliath's spirit as a demonic, supernatural affliction still exists today.

One of Job's friends, Eliphaz, began to wonder where Job's problems came from. He said:

> "Although affliction cometh not forth of the dust, neither doth trouble spring out of the ground." (Job 5:6)

That man was simply perplexed and he began to wonder where on earth Job's problems were coming from. Many of us are like that as we pause and wonder where on earth our problems are springing from. Yet, there must be a source. Goliaths are like that, they make you wonder. Do you know for example, that there are sicknesses that no medical diagnosis, no matter how sophisticated can detect or understand? The current SARS disease, killing people like rats in some parts of the world is a good example. Doctors may keep on telling you they can find nothing wrong with you, yet you know something is wrong but they can see no evidence of any disease. But I tell you there is something and you must do something about that inexplicable "something." Let me give you a couple of testimonies.

One day, a young man came in to see me and he was complaining of hearing strange voices. He was the only one who could hear these voices. He pointed out to me that whoever was speaking to him had nothing pleasant to say. He also said that he could feel some kind of presence around him. He was getting very uncomfortable so he went to the hospital several times. Of course, the doctor could not hear or see anything; no stethoscope could detect anything. So they could not find anything wrong with the man. Unfortunately, the man's wife did not believe in spiritual warfare. This was no small hindrance to effective intercession. Sadly, the case ended in the death of this man. A case of Goliath having his way?

I remember another case of a young, highly skilled and enterprising man. He became unemployed and for some inexplicable reason, he remained in this state for over a year despite very active efforts to secure another job. He made several applications for jobs that yielded no positive results.

Eventually, out of desperation, he applied for a job that required no skill at all to carry out the work. Imagine what effect this had on the man who was highly skilled applying for a job that anybody with no training at all could do. He was invited for an interview which resulted in a formal reply which said "Sorry, we cannot offer you a job this time." In anger, he asked them what he had done wrong at the interview. But sadly, no tangible explanation could be offered.

That afternoon, he rushed to my office, straight from the interview. He said "Pastor, there is a mark! Pastor, there is a mark!" I asked "where is the mark and what mark?" He said he was now persuaded that there was a mark of rejection upon him. Then he went ahead to narrate his latest experience. I knew there and then that this man had recognised his Goliath and he was ready to battle against him.

I recommended that we go into prayer and fasting with night vigils. We did this for a few days and his wife was fully involved also. We broke through in the spirit and by the power of God we killed his Goliath. Two weeks after our GKP vigils, employers began to chase him about for jobs relevant to his skill and his new problem was which job to choose. For over a year, he couldn't understand why he could not secure a job inspite of his skills; but a day came when the snare was broken. **Today, every snare of Goliath in your life is broken in the name of Jesus.**

"Blessed be the Lord, who hath not given us as a prey to

their teeth. Our soul is escaped as a bird out of the snare of the fowlers: the snare is broken and we are escaped." (Ps. 124:6-7)

Let me repeat for emphasis: **Goliath is not of this world!** It is over four years now since the "Goliath of barrenness" died in my marriage. Even then, I still remember vividly many of the events of those waiting years. Some of them are documented in the book "None Shall Be Barren." I want to mention one here to illustrate the point being made.

A few years into our marriage, the Lord began to open my wife's eyes to some unusual events taking place in her dream life. She observed over a period of months that a strange being would try to assault her sexually in the dream. This usually happened at about a week before the due date of her menstruation. Shortly after such an experience, her blood flow would begin. We began to link this strange pattern to her inability to get pregnant.

Medical experts classify an experience such as this as nonsense. To link it with inability to conceive would be gross absurdity. However, we know that *"Spiritual things are spiritually discerned."* Goliath-like experiences such as this are not of this world. It took violent prayers with fasting to uproot this 'monster' from our marriage. (1Cor. 2:14) The fact that this incident ceased after those 'Golaith Killing Prayer

Operations' prove that it was not an experience to be glossed over. And many people are doing just that in their present seemingly hopeless situation. They are committing what I call 'spiritual suicide'!

DIVINE PRESCRIPTION

When you realize that Goliath is not of this world, you will not begin to look for carnal weapons such as medical prescriptions to deal with him. But rather you will seek divine prescriptions. The Bible says:

> "For the weapons of our warfare are not carnal, but mighty through God to the pulling down of strongholds." (llCor. 10:4)

David, who knew the stuff Goliath was made of declared to the giant:

> "And all this assembly shall know that the Lord saveth not with sword and spear: for the battle is the Lord's and He will give you into our hands." (1Samuel 17:47)

All the Israelites soldiers were armed with swords and spears. No wonder none of them could advance against Goliath. It took a man who recognised divine prescription to tell them they all had the wrong weapons. How often do we employ the wrong strategy to fight the right battle. What you need in your life is divine prescription to solve any problem.

Therefore stop looking at Goliath as one ordinary human being out to fight you but rather, see him really as he is, a territorial giant, seeking to dominate a whole nation and her people. The only language he understands is spiritual warfare, he doesn't believe in the decent rules of war. That was why he challenged Israel to a one-to-one combat. God says:

> *"For we wrestle not against flesh and blood, but against powers, against principalities, rulers of the darkness of this world and spiritual wickedness in high places." (Ephesian 6:12)*

Get ready to pray now.

PRAYER ARROWS

➤ *Lord, I repent from every sin that has invited Goliath into my life in the name of Jesus.*

➤ *Father, give me the eyes of Elisha to see beyond the ordinary in the name of Jesus.*

➤ *O Lord, show me great and mighty things which I do not know in the name of Jesus.*

➤ *The Lord who reveals the deep and secret things, come and be my God in the name of Jesus.*

➤ *Holy Spirit, expose every power using the covering of darkness to work against me in the name of Jesus.*

WHO IS GOLIATH?

- Lord, deliver me from every spiritual ignorance in the name of Jesus.

- Let the blood of Jesus flush out of my system every sickness defying medical solution in the name of Jesus.

- I receive by faith, divine prescription to every problem of my life in the name of Jesus.

- I silence every voice of strangers sounding evil into my ears in the name of Jesus.

- I paralyse every demon attacking me in my dreams in the name of Jesus.

- Let the blood of Jesus erase every invisible mark of affliction from my life in the name of Jesus.

- Every problem tagged "inexplicable", receive fire right now in the name of Jesus.

- Lord, give me remarkable breakthroughs and notable miracles this year in the name of Jesus.

- Henceforth, let no one trouble me for I bear in my body the mark of the Lord Jesus Christ.

- Every territorial giant seeking dominion over me, collapse and die in the name of Jesus.

- Thank you Lord for giving me victory on the cross. AMEN.

Chapter Three

GOLIATH INSTILLS FEAR

"And when Saul and all Israel heard those words of the Philistine, they were dismayed and greatly afraid"
1Sam. 17:11

Who is Goliath? Any situation that instils fear in you, great and dreadful fears, is a Goliath. Many people are afraid of other human beings, for whatever reason. There are wives who are living in constant fear of their husbands and vice versa. Yes, there are husbands who are afraid of their wives. Statistics show a large percentage of the population of men in the U.K regularly get beaten by their wives. If you are the wife and are afraid of your husband, you are married to a Goliath. If on the other hand, you are the husband living in the fear of your wife, you have Mrs Jezebel in your house! Either way, both must be defeated with GKPs.

Some people are afraid of their bosses in the office. It is wise to consider that either you are the problem or your boss is the problem. If you search yourself very well and decide that you are not the problem, then whatever makes you to be afraid of your boss is a Goliath and it is time to deal with it.

FEAR OF THE UNKNOWN

There are people who are afraid of problems that have not occured but have merely been pre-concieved in their minds. Often they develop ulcers due to worrying incessantly on what may or may not come to pass, this is usually called fear of the unknown. This happened to me many years ago when I was at university.

During my time as a Students' Union leader at the then University of Ife (Now Obafemi Awolowo University) in Nigeria, there was a major crisis involving all university students and the country's government. The government withdrew subsidies on university education and we, the students, would have none of that. We began a 'war' with the government. I was one of the students' leaders in the forefront of the campaign and whilst I dared not betray the students, at the same time I was afraid of many things that MAY OR MAY NOT HAPPEN.

Primarily, I was afraid of the possibility of being expelled from the University. What will I tell my poor parents. I was also afraid of the possibility of some of our demonstrations becoming violent and the police killing me or other students I was leading as I remember previous demonstrations held by the nation's students' had led to numerous deaths. Another fear was being arrested by the notoriously brutal state security agents. The military was in power then and they could have thrown me in some dingy detention forever. My fears were further heightened by the daunting question, "What if I die?" This was how Goliath bombarded me with all sorts of fears of the unknown.

The result was that I developed a sickness doctors called 'Duodenal Ulcer'. I still remember vividly asking the doctor what causes Duodenal Ulcer. He told me in simple terms: 'fear, worries and anxieties' were the primary causes. As he told me this, I looked back at the last one month of my life and recalled that those words BEST described my life. "FEAR, WORRIES AND ANXIETIES." For the next six months, I was on medical prescriptions treating duodenal ulcer.

Question: Did my entire fears come to pass?

Answer: No. I suffered for nothing! Are you like that today? There is a sure treatment that I did not have at that time. Jesus Christ is that all time treatment. The Bible, which I did not believe in then as I was a Muslim says:

> *"Don't worry about anything; instead, pray about everything; tell God your needs and don't forget to thank Him for His answers. If you do this you will experience God's peace, which is far more wonderful than the human mind can understand. His peace will keep your thoughts and your hearts quiet and at rest as you trust in Christ Jesus." (Phil. 4:6-7 Living Bible).*

Someone called this "Philliprine capsule." Whatever you call it, I can tell you it works wonders if you take it regularly.

Do you remember the man called Job? Do you know one of the reasons why satan got him so cheaply? I will tell you, It was due to his own self imposed fear. The fear of the unknown. Listen to him:

> *"For the thing which I greatly feared is come upon me, and that which I was afraid of is come unto me." (Job 3:25)*

There it is! Job's problem started with the fear of what had not even taken place. The demonic supernatural began to work on his fears, because he had sent messages into the spirit realm via the channel of fear. It was just a matter of time before what he feared began to manifest in reality.

In simple terms, the truth here is that if you are afraid of illness, it is very likely you will soon fall ill. If you are afraid of death, 'Mr Death' is probably not far away. Now you see how serious the matter is. If you do not kill fear, fear will kill you. Goliath carries fear, so kill him quickly!

"For as he thinketh in his heart so is he..." (Prov. 23:7)

I will give you another real example of fear of the unknown. The Pastor of the largest single congregation in the world, Pastor David Yongi Cho once became a victim of this dangerous spirit.

Before Pastor Cho met Jesus, he had an experience one day in the classroom as a biology student. The teacher said "Those who have long necks are more prone to contact tuberculosis." Everyone looked round at each other's neck to see who had a longer than average one. It was clear that Yongi Cho had the longest neck. From that very moment, this young man developed the fear that he might one day suffer tuberculosis.

Not long after, he indeed collapsed one day and ended up in hospital with not suprisingly, the disease, Tuberculosis. To make matters worse, the doctors told Yongi Cho, he only had at the very most four months to live? Please pray this prayer NOW:

Every evil word spoken into the air concerning me, be nullified right now in the name of Jesus!

It took the encounter with Jesus to deliver Yongi Cho from the evil death sentence passed upon him. **I cancel** every decree of sickness and death hanging over you in the name of Jesus.

GOLIATH AND JEZEBEL

Goliath carries a spirit similar in some respect to that of Jezebel. Everybody was afraid of Jezebel including her husband, Ahab. Even a prophet of God, Elijah, who had just seen God send fire at Mount Carmel, upon his request was more afraid of Jezebel than the God that 'answereth by fire'! Read what transpired:

> *"And Ahab told Jezebel all that Elijah had done and withal how he had slain all the prophets with the sword.*
>
> *Then Jezebel sent a messenger unto Elijah, saying, so let the gods do to me, and more also, if I make not thy life as the life of one of them by tomorrow about this time.*
>
> *And when he saw that, he arose and went for his life, and came to Beer-sheba, which belongeth to Judah, and left his servant there.*
>
> *But he himself went a day's journey into the wilderness and came and sat down under a juniper tree and he requested for himself that he might die and said it is enough now O Lord, take away my life; for I am not better than my fathers." (1Kings 19:1-4)*

Look at Elijah. As a result of the fear of one human

being, he suffered several things. Amongst them are:

1. He was intimidated and overwhelmed.

2. He became confused and controlled by fear.

3. He suffered the spirit of death wish and suicidal tendencies.

4. He immediately lost his vision and focus. He began a purposeless journey into the wilderness.

5. He lost touch with God and His saving powers.

6. The spirit of weariness and tiredness consumed him.

7. Elijah, the fire prophet began to suffer from low self esteem. He said "for I am not better than my fathers." I ask, which of his fathers ever called for and received fire from heaven or slew eight hundred and fifty prophets of Baal in one day?

8. He began to sleep what I call the 'sleep of death.' But for the 'manna' from heaven, he probably would have slept himself to eternity.

9. The arrow of divination and witchcraft penetrated into his soul.

10. He suffered mental paralysis.

11. He suffered unfulfilled destiny. He was replaced before his time.

WHO IS GOLIATH?
FEAR: THE DESTINY TERMINATOR

See what fear can do to man. If a man of Elijah's calibre could suffer all those afflictions because of fear, then you can begin to appreciate the evil consequences of fear. No wonder God speaks to us so much about fear.

> *"The fear of man bringeth a snare: but whoso putteth his trust in the Lord shall be safe."* (Prov. 29:25)

The fear of Goliath was a snare to Israel and so will the fear of any man be to you if you do not deal with it now. Saul, a whole king, became afraid of an uncircumcised Philistine!

> *"When Saul and all Israel heard those words of the Philistine, (Goliath) they were dismayed and greatly afraid. And all the men of Israel when they saw the man,(Goliath), fled from him, and were sore afraid."* (1Samuel. 17:11 & 24) (Emphasis author's)

Can you see King Saul running away? I am sure his crown fell off in one direction as he fled and he threw away his royal staff, his royal garment was not helping the race, so he cast it off also. The Philistines were laughing all the way!

Fear is a destiny terminator. That was what happened to a whole generation of Israel who perished in the wilderness. It was fear and God warned them against it as they were approaching the Promised Land. But alas! they did not heed His warning.

> *"Only rebel not ye against the Lord, neither fear ye the people of the land; for they are bread for us: their defence is departed from them, and the Lord is with us: fear them not." (Num.14:9)*

If only you know that Goliath is bread for you, you will not be afraid of 'giant-like' problems again. Just look at the way Goliath eventually died. If anyone had told Saul that only one stone (not even spear or sword) would completely destroy the giant, I would love to imagine what effect that would have had on his fear. No wonder they say, FEAR is "False Evidence Appearing Real." Why must you allow your destiny to be ruined by such falsehood!

> *"But the men that went up with him said, we be not able to go up against the people for they are stronger than we.*
>
> *And they brought up an evil report of the land which they had searched unto the children of Israel, saying, the land, through which we have gone to search it is a land that eateth up the inhabitants thereof, and all the people that we saw in it are men of a great stature. And there we saw the giants, the sons of Anak, which come of the giants: and we were in our own sight as grasshoppers, and so we were in their sight." (Numbers 13:31-33)*

WHO IS GOLIATH?

Those ten men developed this grasshopper mentality out of fear of the giants they saw ahead of them. That mentality is the same spirit of low self-esteem that came upon Elijah for fear of Jezebel. The tragic consequence of these men's mentality was that it became infectious. A whole generation was infected with this hydra- headed disease and they perished without entering into their inheritance. Moses warned them but they would not listen. Read what he said:

> "Then I said unto you, Dread not, neither be afraid of them....Yet in this thing ye did not believe the Lord your God." (Deut. 1:29 & 32)

Fear is a destiny killer. Fear breeds limitation. Fear prevents fulfillment. Fear causes stagnation. Fear hinders progress. Fear opposes breakthrough. Fear paralyses vision. Fear denies God and enthrones satan. Fear destroys potential. Fear dislocates and dispossesses. Whatever the goal of fear is in man, it is negative. Goliath carries all the burden of fear but before he dumps them on you, you must kill him quickly. God hates fear. That is why He tells us three hundred and sixty five times in the Bible that we should 'fear not.' He has an anti-fear capsule for each day of the year! Glory to God!

> "But now thus saith the Lord that created thee...and he that formed thee...Fear not; for I have redeemed thee, I have called thee by thy name; thou art mine. When thou

> *passeth through the waters, I will be with thee; and through the rivers, they shall not overflow thee: when thou walkest through the fire, thou shall not be burned; neither shall the flame kindle upon thee."(Isaiah 43:1-2)*

The reason why many do not experience God's miraculous power is because of fear. They are afraid to declare God's words and stand on them. For example, many believers are afraid to lay hands on the sick and say to them *"You are healed in the name of Jesus."* Why? They say to themselves, *"What if the person does not get healed."* They are proceeding with the mind set of fear. This is wrong thinking. What if the person gets healed? Now we know why the early Christians prayed for boldness, they knew the danger of fear so they prayed for its opposite: BOLDNESS.

> *"And now, Lord, behold their threatenings: and grant unto thy servants, that with all boldness they may speak thy word." (Acts 4:29)*

God loves you when you pray like that. Oh, He answered those Christians instantly. In *verse 31*, their prayer was answered:

> *"And when they had prayed, the place was shaken where they were assembled together; and they were all filled with the Holy Ghost, and they spake the word of God with boldness."*

FEAR QUENCHES MIRACLES

Some people who are already experiencing miracles lose it because of sudden bursts of fear. The Apostle Peter, began to walk on water (a miracle), but he fell into this fit of fear and so began to sink.

> *"And in the fourth watch of the night Jesus went onto them, walking on the sea. And when the disciples saw him walking on the sea, they were troubled saying, it is a spirit and they cried out for fear. But straightaway Jesus spake unto them saying be of good cheer it is I be not afraid. And Peter answered him and said Lord, if it be thou bid me come unto thee on the water. And He said Come. And when Peter was come down out of the ship, he walked on the water, to go to Jesus. But when he saw the wind boisterous, he was afraid and beginning to sink, he cried, saying, Lord save me."* (Matt. 14:25-30)

Many people have answered the call of Jesus Christ. They are born again and growing in the faith, experiencing miracles (walking on water). But then, boisterous winds come in the form of trials, temptations and the storms of life. These evil wind came to frighten them. They yield to the fear and begin to backslide (sink).

Today, if you are like that, all you need to do is to cry to Jesus, like Peter did and say, "Lord save me." I assure you, He will stretch forth His hand and catch you into His glorious, powerful and reassuring embrace.

Let us pause now and fire some deadly arrows against the fear carrying Goliath. Remember this scripture as you pray:

> *"For God hath not given us the spirit of fear; but of power, and of love and of a sound mind." (2Tim. 1:7)*

PRAYER ARROWS:

▶ *Father, I thank you for exposing every lie of the enemy that has been enslaving me.*

▶ *Every fear, real or imagined, I come against you in the name of Jesus.*

▶ *I overthrow the throne of fear in my life in the name of Jesus.*

▶ *In the name of Jesus, I receive deliverance from the spirit of fear.*

▶ *Lord, lay your hand of glory upon me and baptise me with the spirit of boldness in the name of Jesus.*

▶ *I refuse to allow fear to abort and destroy my destiny in the name of Jesus.*

▶ *I paralyse every Goliath instilling fear into my life in the name of Jesus.*

WHO IS GOLIATH?

- *Every fear of the unknown, melt away in the name of Jesus.*

- *Let the peace of God keep my heart and mind at rest in the name of Jesus.*

- *Father forgive me for the sins of fear, doubt and unbelief in the name of Jesus.*

- *I command every snare of fear fashioned against me to break now in the name of Jesus.*

- *I release my soul from the snare of fear in the name of Jesus.*

- *I reject the spirit of fear and receive the spirit of power and sound mind in the name of Jesus.*

- *I reject the fear of failure in the name of Jesus.*

- *I reject the fear of sickness in the name of Jesus.*
- *I reject the fear of death in the name of Jesus.*

- *I receive power to confront my fears and overcome them in the name of Jesus. I overcome every satanic fear by the blood of Jesus.*

- *Lord, baptise me with the Jehu anointing to destroy every hand of Jezebel in the name of Jesus.*

- *I declare that the threats of Goliath will not come to pass in the name of Jesus.*

- *Let every fear of terrorist attack over my nation melt away in the name of Jesus.*

- *I decree that terrorists will not fire a single missile upon my city in the name of Jesus.*

- *Lord send confusion into the midst of terrorist gangs plotting against our nation in the name of Jesus.*

- *I shall not be afraid for the terror by night nor for the arrow that flieth by day in the name of Jesus.*

- *Every sickness and infirmity caused by fears, be healed now in the name of Jesus.*

- *I receive deliverance from every fear of repeated tragedies in the name of Jesus.*

- *Let my fear of the past be buried with the past in the name of Jesus.*

- *Lord save me from sinking in the river of fear in the name of Jesus. AMEN.*

Chapter Four

GOLIATH IS A REPROACH

"And David spake to the men that stood by him, saying, what shall be done to the man that killeth this Philistine, and taketh away the reproach from Israel? For who is this uncircumcised Philistine, that he should defy the armies of the living God?" 1 Sam. 17:26

Who is Goliath? Goliath is any situation that brings a reproach, disgrace or shame to you, your family or your nation. In describing Goliath, the men of Israel said, the man Goliath, came to defy Israel, as he challenged Israel to open combat. The fear of this giant brought shame and disgrace to a whole nation.

The enemy is constantly challenging you with problems and the fear of them. If you are a believer, he wants to disgrace you and put you to shame; he wants to ridicule you and your God and he desires that you become so overwhelmed by his presence that you succumb to his threats, deny your God and become his slave. When the shame of satanic attack came upon Job, listen to what his wife said:

> *"Then said his wife unto him. Dost thou still retain thine integrity? Curse God, and die." (Job 2:9)*

NATIONAL REPROACH

That is the mission of Goliath. He is out to tell you that God cannot save you so you had better bury your head in shame. That is precisely what happened to Judah when Hezekiah was king. Senacherib, the king of Assyria, had the spirit of Goliath in him. He sent several threatening messages to the people of Judah and their king.

> *"Neither let Hezekiah make you trust in the Lord, saying, the Lord will surely deliver us: this city shall not be delivered into the hand of the king of Assyria.*
>
> *Hearken not to Hezekiah: for thus saith the King of Assyria, make an agreement with me by a present, and come out to me and eat ye every one of his vine, and every one of his fig tree, and drink ye every one of the waters of his own cistern;*
>
> *Until I come and take you away to a land like your own land, a land of corn and wine a land of bread and vineyards.*

WHO IS GOLIATH?

Beware lest Hezekiah persuade you, saying the Lord will deliver us. Hath any of the gods of the nations delivered his land out of the hand of the king of Assyria? (Isaiah 36:15-18)

The greatest shame and disgrace is to enter into an agreement with an unrepentant enemy as it surely leads to enslavement. King Hezekiah knew what to do about this reproach. He went into his closet and laid the enemy's threats before God and there he prayed, what I call 'Goliath Killing Prayers'.

"And Hezekiah received the letter from the hand of the messengers, and read it; and Hezekiah went up unto the house of the Lord, and spread it before the Lord. And Hezekiah prayed unto the Lord..." (Isaiah 37:14-15)

Result: The Lord took over the battle. He spoke concerning the situation and subsequently He acted and took away the reproach.

"Therefore thus saith the Lord concerning the king of Assyria, He shall not come into this city, nor shoot an arrow there, nor come before it with shields, nor cast a bank against it.

By the way that he came, by the same way shall he return, and shall not come into this city, thus saith the Lord. For I will defend this city to save it for mine own sake, and for my servant David's sake." (Isa. 37:33-35)

We have been using this scripture lately in our church to pray for our city and nation. The threat of terrorist attacks on major cities of Great Britain can be likened to the threat of Senacherib of Assyria. Of late, the threats have become so real, so much so that the government even began to prepare everybody's mind for an attack, saying that it was not a question of whether there will be an attack, but a question of when. Nobody thought of preventing it or at least, it was not reported by the media. Not many of our leaders in government appear to believe that there is a God who can 'defend our city'; who can ensure that not a single 'arrow' (missile) is fired into London and One who can make sure that every terrorist turn back the same way he came and never step into this 'city'.

Our Prime Minister has not called a day of National Prayer and Fasting to 'spread' the threat of 'Al Qaeda' before God and cry to Him to take away the reproach of wickedness. It is sad when we forget our God and begin to serve the god of Goliath. (You might recall that during Churchills days as prime minister, he called a national day of prayer in 1940 May 26th, just before the battle of Dunkirk. Within 24hours, God intervened miraculously to save the British troops from Hitler's offensive).

"The wicked shall be turned into hell and all the nations that forget God." (Ps. 9:17)

WHO IS GOLIATH?

"Blessed is the nation whose God is the Lord; and the people whom he hath chosen for his own inheritance. The Lord looketh from heaven; he beholdeth all the sons of men. From the place of his habitation he looketh upon all the inhabitants of the earth.

He fashioneth their hearts alike; he considereth all their works.

There is no king saved by the multitude of an host: a mighty man is not delivered by much strength. An horse is a vain thing for safety: neither shall he deliver any by his great strength.

Behold the eye of the Lord is upon them that fear him, upon them that hope in his mercy. To deliver their soul from death, and to keep them alive in famine." (Ps.33:12-19)

The time is now! Our nation should return to God, seek Him, call upon Him and experience His mighty move in us and against the enemy.

"Righteousness exalteth a nation, but sin is a reproach to any people." (Prov. 14:34)

When God speaks, He says what He means and He means what He says. He also has the power and the ability to bring what He says to pass. When King Hezekiah prayed, God heard and took over the battle. The nation of Judah did not have to lift a finger.

> *"Then the angel of the Lord went forth and smote in the camp of the Assyrians a hundred and fourscore and five thousand: and when they arose early in the morning, behold they were all dead corpses."* (Isa. 37:36)

In fact, Senacherib, the king of Assyria was killed by his own sons.

> *"And it came to pass as he (Senacherib) was worshipping in the house of Nisroch his god, that Adrammelech and Sharezer his sons smote him with the sword..."* (Isa.37:38)

There is something to learn from the destruction of Senacherib. He was busy worshipping his god, an idol! If only our leaders could become busy worshipping the living God who is the Rock of this nation.

> *"And such as do wickedly against the covenant shall He corrupt by flatteries: but the people that do know their God shall be strong, and do exploits."* (Dan.11:32)

Goliath wants to bring reproach, shame and ridicule upon the individual, city and nation. What is needed in order to overcome this is a Davidic army of worshippers, intercessors and prayer warriors to deal with his onslaught.

PERSONAL REPROACH

Whatever is behind your reproach, if you pray today, you will have testimonies in the name of Jesus. A reproach was upon Rachel, the wife of Jacob. She cried and was heard in heaven.

> *"And God remembered Rachel, and God hearkened to her, and opened her womb. And she concieved and bare a son; and said, God hath taken away my reproach." (Gen. 30:22-23)*

In the same vein, God will take away every reproach of your life this year in the name of Jesus.

Another couple in the Bible had this Goliath reproach upon them. They were Zacharia and Elizabeth. All medical evidence proved that they would live and die in their reproach of barrenness. But who can write you off when God writes you in? They sought God, prayed to Him, walked in His commandment and were righteous before Him. Divine intervention came and the reproach became a thing of the past. In Luke 1: 24-25, we read:

> *"And after those days, (of concentrated worship and prayers) his wife Elizabeth concieved, and hid herself five months, saying, thus hath the Lord dealt with me in the days wherein he looked on me, to take away my reproach among men." (Authors emphasis in brackets)*

As previously mentioned in this book, for several

years, my wife and I were not able to have a child despite several medical and 'extra-medical' attempts. 'Experts' *ruled out* any possibility of us having a child. But God *ruled in* the possibility and took away the reproach. Now we have two miracle boys to the Glory of God!

The Lord that did all these miracles is not dead and has not changed. He is still able to do even much more than these for YOU!

> *"Now unto him that is able to do exceedingly, aboundantly above all that we ask or think, according to the power that worketh in us..." (Eph. 3:20)*

> *"Jesus Christ the same yesterday, and today, and for ever." (Heb.13:8)*

REPROACH AND CIRCUMCISION

David said in 1Sam. 17:26 "...What shall be done to the man that killeth this Philistine and taketh away the reproach from Israel? For who is this uncircumcised Philistine, that he should defy the armies of the living God?"

Back then, it was considered a disgrace for an uncircumcised Goliath to challenge the circumcised Israel to battle. David was in fact, speaking the mind of God. To be uncircumcised in the wider sense is a reproach in the sight of God.

When they had crossed the River Jordan, God instructed Joshua to circumcise the children of Israel the second time.

> *"At that time the Lord said unto Joshua, make thee sharp knives, and circumcise again the children of Israel the second time." (Josh.5:2)*

Joshua obeyed and the children of Israel went through the pains and rigours of circumcision. Thereafter God said:

> *"...This day have I rolled away the reproach of Egypt from off you. Wherefore the name of the place is called Gilgal unto this day." Verse 9*

What is God saying to us in all this? The uncircumcised Goliath is a reproach. Those who want to get rid of him must themselves be circumcised. Are you circumcised? Not of the flesh, but of the heart.

> *"And the Lord thy God will circumcise thine heart, and the heart of thy seed, to love the Lord thy God with all thine heart, and with all thy soul, that thou mayest live." (Deut. 30:6)*

> *"...and circumcision is that of the heart, in the spirit, and not in the letter..." (Rom. 2:29)*

> "In whom also ye are circumcised with the circumcision made without hands, in putting off the body of the sins of the flesh by the circumcision of Christ…And you being dead in your sins and the uncircumcision of your flesh, hath he quickened together with him having forgiven you all trespasses; blotting out the handwriting of ordinances that was against us, which was contrary to us, and took it out of the way, nailing it to his cross." (Col. 2:11,13-14)

Jesus Christ died for us so that our hearts might be circumcised. Sin is a reproach. *(Proverbs 14:34)* When the heart is not circumcised, it serves and gratifies sins, which in turn leads to shame and disgrace. When you come to Jesus and you are in Christ, you will experience the 'sharp knife' of Joshua, a type of Jesus (the Saviour). His 'sharp knife' will circumcise you and make you too tough for your Goliath.

> "Who shall separate us from the love of Christ? Shall tribulation, or distress, or persecution, or famine, or nakedness, or peril, or sword?…Nay in all these things we are more than conquerors through him that loved us." (Rom. 8:35,37)

Goliath is a champion (i.e. a conqueror), but God says in the scripture above that you are more powerful than him through Jesus Christ that loves you.

PRAYER ARROWS

 Thank you Father, for it is your will to rid my life of every reproach.

WHO IS GOLIATH?

- Lord, I confess every sin that has brought a reproach to my life and I repent from them in the name of Jesus.

- Lord Jesus, come into my heart, circumcise me wholly.

- Father, I stand in gap for my nation, I confess that our sins have brought the reproach of the enemy upon us.

- Lord, revive us again and cause your glory to shine upon our land in the name of Jesus.

- Father, rend the heavens and cause the rain of mercy to fall upon your people in the name of Jesus.

- Let every power challenging the power of my God crumble in the name of Jesus.

- Let every garment of shame and reproach be burnt to ashes in the name of Jesus.

- Lord, hear my cry and take away my reproach in the name of Jesus.

- I refuse to be a slave to sin and to serve the god of Goliath in the name of Jesus.

- Let the blood of Jesus wipe off every mark of reproach from my life in the name of Jesus.

- Father, give me the grace to endure your 'sharp knife' and be saved to the end in the name of Jesus.

➤ *I declare that I am greater than any Goliath because of Christ that is in me.*

➤ *I strongly confess that I am more than a conqueror in the name of Jesus. Thank you Lord for setting me free from shame and sorrow.*

Chapter Five

GOLIATH IS A GIANT OBSTACLE

"But David went and returned from Saul to feed his father's sheep at Bethlehem" 1Sam. 17:15

ANOINTED TO REIGN

In *1Samuel 16*, God rejected Saul from reigning over Israel and He chose David to reign in his stead. God's choice was sealed by the anointing 'service' performed by Samuel. The service took place at the house of Jesse, the father of David:

> *"Then Samuel took the horn of oil, and anointed him in the midst of his brethren and the Spirit of the Lord came upon David from that day forward. So Samuel rose up and went to Ramah." (1Sam.16:13)*

As soon as the service was over, David's journey to the palace began. The anointing began to make ways for him. When the Spirit of the Lord is upon you, doors hitherto shut begin to open. When the Lord anoints you, the oil of favour rests upon you. That was what happened to David. All of a sudden they began to notice him where no one took notice of him before. **This year, I prophesy that people will notice you in places you least expect in the name of Jesus.**

A few verses after his anointing, David made his way to the palace not by any personal publicity or distribution of complimentary cards. But by divine advertisement.

> *"Wherefore, Saul sent messengers unto Jesse, and said, send me David thy son, which is with the sheep…And David came to Saul, and stood before him; and he loved him greatly; and he became his armour bearer. And Saul sent to Jesse, saying, Let David, I pray thee, stand before me; for he hath found favour in my sight." (1Sam.16: 19,21-22)*

That was how David left the company of sheep and found himself in the company of chiefs. He was diligent with the sheep, and was thereby promoted to be with the chiefs.

> *"Seest thou a man diligent in his business? He shall stand before kings; he shall not stand before mean men." (Prov. 22:29)*

Your journey from 'Shepherd-Bush' to 'Palace Square' is about to begin. If you have not given your life to Christ, why not do so right now and let the

Spirit of the Lord come upon you from this day forward. That is the anointing to reign that not even Goliath, try as he may, can take away from you. (Turn to the last page and repeat the prayer in fulness of faith

> "But you are a chosen generation, a royal priesthood, an holy nation, a peculiar people that ye should show forth the praises of him who hath called you out of darkness unto his marvellous light." (1Peter 2:9)

> "If we suffer, we shall also reign with him. If we deny Him, He also will deny us." (2Tim.2:12)

OBSTACLES TO REIGNING.

David had apparently settled down in the palace as King Saul's Amour Bearer. He only had to wait for the appointed time when the baton of rulership would be formally handed over to him. Then all of a sudden, we notice a u-turn.

> "But David went and returned from Saul to feed his father's sheep at Bethlehem." (1Sam.17:15)

What on earth sent the man, David back to 'ShepherdsBush'? That is what I call "Obstacles to Reigning." It is interesting that this was exactly the same time Goliath came on the scene.

Goliath is a satanic agent sent to obstruct God's plan and purpose for your life. He is a destiny killer, a giant obstacle that must be crushed to ensure you reign.

Satan's game plan here was to find a way of killing David quickly and ending his mission on earth. Goliath was his perfect weapon for this goal, and Goliath was going to do a good job of it. Hear what he said when he saw David.

> *"And the Philistine said unto David, am I a dog, that thou comest to me with staves? And the Philistine cursed David by his gods. And the Philistine said to David, come to me, and I will give thy flesh unto the fowls of the air, and to the beasts of the field".* (1Sam.17:43-44)

Now, you must understand that those were no ordinary threats. Witchcraft was already in operation. Goliath uttered some powerful satanic incantation in the name of his gods; he actually cursed David. For an ordinary person, that would have been the end of the matter, that curse alone was sufficient to finish David. He could have just dropped dead! But David was still standing strong. That is not a light thing. Why did David not drop dead at the power of this curse? Simple: Power surpasses power.

> *"He suffered no man to do them wrong…saying touch not mine anointed and do my prophets no harm."* (Ps. 105:11)

WHO IS GOLIATH?

David was already anointed at the time Goliath was issuing out a curse against him. The curse did not work because of the operation of the settled word of God in favour of David.

When Balak, the king of Moab wanted Balaam, the diviner to curse Israel, he met with similar failure. Balaam in the face of his difficulties in cursing Israel declared:

> "How shall I curse whom God hath not cursed? Or how shall I defy whom the Lord hath not defied?...God is not a man, that he should lie; neither the son of man. that he should repent: hath he said, and shall he not do it? Or hath he spoken, and shall he not make it good? Behold I have recieved commandment to bless: and he hath blessed and I cannot reverse it...surely there is no enchantment against Jacob, neither is there any divination against Israel: according to this time it shall be said of Jacob and of Israel, what hath God wrought!" (Numbers 23:8,19,20,23)

I prophesy that henceforth, whoever touches you touches God's eye for you are the apple of His eyes.

"For thus saith The Lord of Hosts; After the glory hath He sent me into the nations which spoiled you:

for he that toucheth you toucheth the apple of His eyes." (Zech. 2:8)

BACK TO THE PALACE.

Whenever the devil is rejoicing at his smartness, he sees God outsmarting him. Goliath actually became David's catalyst to the palace. **May your problem become your ladder of promotion in the name of Jesus.**

Obstacles are problems and they can be as serious as Goliath. However, a child of God must not be afraid of problems. In fact, when you begin to see your problems as the ladder to your promotion, you will begin to prepare yourself for a good climb on it.

David was forgotten as soon as he returned from Saul to feed the sheep. The proof of forgetfulness came when, after David had successfully challenged Goliath, Saul was inquiring whose son David was. In (1Sam.17:55)

> "And when Saul saw David go forth against the Philistine, he said unto Abner, the captain of the host,
>
> Abner, whose son is this youth? And Abner said, As thy soul liveth, O king, I cannot tell."

Alas! How quickly David was forgotten once he left the palace. Granted that Saul was mentally confused and may have suffered from memory failure at this time, consider Abner, the army General, who along with others had watched with admiration, as David played for Saul's recovery. How could Abner have forgoten David? But do not be surprised, it is all part of the enemy's game plan to cause those who will advance your cause to forget you so that you do not fulfil your destiny. However, I have good news for you, the Book of Remembrance is being opened for your sake. **All those who are supposed to help you will begin to become restless until they have risen to their divine duty concerning your life.**

> *"On that night could not the king sleep, and he commanded to bring the book of records of the chronicles; and they were read before the king. And it was found written, that Mordecai had told of Bigthana and Teresh, two of the king's chamberlains, the keepers of the door, who sought to lay hand on the king Ahasuerus. And the king said, what honour and dignity hath been done to Mordecai for this? Then said the King's servants that ministered unto him, there is nothing done for him."*
> *(Esther 6:1-3)*

They had forgotten Mordecai who deserved to be promoted. However, the day God opened the Book of Remembrance for his sake, even the king could not sleep. How did this happen? Obstacle, I repeat, the Obstacle called Haman. If Haman had not risen to oppose Mordecai, his promotion would not have come. If Goliath had not risen to oppose David, and if David had not overcome this obstacle, he would never have returned to the palace. In order to reign in the palace, you must rule on the battlefield.

As it turned out, the Goliath encounter gave David a divine advertisement. This obstacle created the way for a return to the palace and the return was so glorious that king Saul shut the door to his exit from the palace.

> "And Saul took him that day, and would let him go no more home to his father's house." (1Sam.18:2)

If the enemy knew this was how it would all turn out, he would not have set Goliath against David.

> "But we speak the wisdom of God in a mystery, even the hidden wisdom, which God ordained before the world unto our glory. Which none of the princes of this world know, for had they know it, they would not have crucified the Lord of glory. But as it is written, eye hath not seen, nor ear heard, neither have entered into the heart of man, the things which God hath prepared for them that love him.." 1Cor. 2:7-9)

Rest assured that hidden in your opposition is an opportunity; in your trial is a triumph, in your test, is a testimony, in your adversity is an advantage and in your story is a glory. Pray now that the Lord will anoint your eyes that you may see these great and mighty things that He has prepared for you.

WHO IS GOLIATH?

"I counsel thee to ...anoint thine eyes with eyesalve, that thou mayest see." (Rev. 3:18)

PRAYER ARROWS

➤ Father, I praise you because you anointed Jesus with the oil of gladness above His contemporaries.

➤ I declare today that I am the apple of God's eyes, therefore whoever touches me touches God's eyes.

➤ Lord, I will not fall from grace to grass in the name of Jesus.

➤ Every power putting my destiny in reverse gear, fall down and die in the name of Jesus.

➤ Lord, anoint my head with fresh oil in the name of Jesus.

➤ Lord, exalt my horn like the horn of an unicorn in the name of Jesus.

➤ Father, let the Holy Spirit be permanently resident in me in the name of Jesus.

➤ I repent from every sin that grieves the Holy Spirit and I separate myself from those sin forever in the name of Jesus.

➤ O God of righteousness, make it impossible for me to backslide in the name of Jesus.

➤ Lord, anoint me with the oil of favour in the name of Jesus.

- Today, I receive the 'forget-me-not' oil upon my life in the name of Jesus.

- Father, give me a diligent spirit and let me stand before kings in the name of Jesus.

- Lord God, make me an unrepentant witness of your resurrection power in the name of Jesus.

- Goliath, David (put your name here) is coming, get out of the way or be crushed to death in the name of Jesus.

- Lord, catapult me from the company of sheep into the fellowship of chiefs in the name of Jesus.

- Father, don't allow my crown to go to another, let me reign with Jesus, your dear Son and my Saviour.

- Let my obstacle become my ride to promotion in the name of Jesus.

- Let every satanic gameplan to rob me of my destiny be nullified in the name of Jesus.

- I declare that no enchantment shall stand against me and no divination shall come to pass concerning me in the name of Jesus.

- Let every incantation uttered against me under the instrumentality of the wind, the water, the air and the earth become as nothing in the name of Jesus.

WHO IS GOLIATH?

▶ Lord this year, cause those that matter to remember me for good in the name of Jesus.

▶ Father, anoint my head with oil in the presence of my enemies in the name of Jesus.

▶ Let every Goliath obstructing the peace of our nation be subdued in the name of Jesus.

▶ Let every encounter with problems result in my promotion in the name of Jesus.

▶ Father, open my eyes to see the opportunity in my opposition, the triumph in my trial and the testimonies in my tests in the name of Jesus.

▶ Thank you Lord, for appointing me to reign with you. AMEN.

PART

2

GOLIATH KILLING PRAYERS (GKP)

Overcoming The Giants Of Your Life

In the first part of this book, we saw the character and identity of Goliath. When your problem is revealed, solution is just around the corner. We now understand that Goliath is a stubborn problem; he is not of this world, he instils fear; he is a reproach and he is also a giant obstacle to the fulfilment of destiny.

Our focus in this second part is on how to deal with Goliath and overcome him and we will examine how David dealt with Goliath. Great lessons will be learnt from the weapons of David. His weapons illustrate many aspects of prayer and spiritual warfare of which we are supposed to engage in as believers in order to overcome our 'giants'- these are 'Goliath

WHO IS GOLIATH?

Killing Prayers'. We are going to see salient ingredients of this devastating prayer and you will be encouraged to incorporate them in your prayer life and undoubtedly begin to enjoy a victorious life.

You may not have a physical Goliath confronting you in the natural and we are not referring to carnal weapons of swords and shields or AK47 and Bazookas. David's strategies for killing Goliath foreshadows or are types of the New Testament believers' strategies for dealing with 'giants' of life. While you may not wrestle with a physical Goliath, you are wrestling with his spiritual equivalent needing equally violent resistance, albeit in the spirit. The Lord tells us in *Ephesian 6:12*

> *"For we wrestle not against flesh and blood, but against principalities, against powers, against the rulers of darkness of this world, against spiritual wickedness in high places."*

When you know what 'wrestling' is you will understand the battle we are up against as Christians. There is no rule of decency in wrestling; it is the battle of the market place and anyone can be hit at any moment, this gives you an idea of how horrible satan is in his opposition to believers, but you have the victory of the cross to remind you that it is written:

> *"And from the days of John the Baptist until now the kingdom of heaven suffereth violence and the violent*

take it by force." (Matt. 11:12)

Let me repeat the important point that our war is not with carnal weapons, not arguments, not screaming at each other, not bitterness and unforgiveness towards one another, not gossip, envy, jealousy and all manner of carnality. Our weapons of prayer are very mighty indeed.

> *"For the weapons of our warfare are not carnal, but mighty through God to the pulling down of strong holds. Casting down imaginations, and every high thing that exalteth itself against the knowledge of God and bringing into captivity every thought to the obedience of Christ."(2Cor. 10:4-5)*

Get ready to understand these weapons of prayer and step up to the challenge, apply them so that you can enjoy all round victory against the 'giants' of your life. Before you read the next chapter, pray the following prayers aloud.

PRAYER ARROWS

▶ *Lord purge me of any carnality in the name of Jesus.*

▶ *Father, lead me to the Rock that is higher than me in the name of Jesus.*

▶ *Father, teach my fingers to fight in the name of Jesus. Lord, give me divine prescriptions to every problem of my life in the name of Jesus.*

WHO IS GOLIATH?

- By faith, I put on the whole armour of God. I wear the belt of truth; I take on the breastplate of righteousness, I wear the shoes of the gospel of peace, the shield of faith is in my hand, the helmet of salvation is upon my head and I am armed with the Sword of the Spirit.

- O Lord, empower me to withstand in the evil day and having done all to stand in the name of Jesus.

- Holy Spirit, help me not to war after the flesh but to war in the spirit in the name of Jesus.

- I confess that I am a soldier of Christ, I therefore receive His grace to fight the good fight of faith in the name of Jesus.

- Let all invisible associates of Goliath be disgraced out of my life in the name of Jesus.

- I withdraw every co-operation or agreement of my flesh with Goliath in the name of Jesus.

- Lord, teach me divine strategies to wage a good warfare in the name of Jesus.

Chapter Six

GKP IS BOLD

"Thy servant slew both the lion and the bear and this uncircumcised Philistine shall be as one of them, seeing he hath defied the armies of the living God." 1Sam.17:36

Goliath Killing Prayers, like any effective prayers, must have an element of boldness. You cannot overcome a giant obstacle through acts of cowardice. In *Proverbs 28:1*, the Bible says:

> *"The coward flees when no one is pursuing but the righteous are as bold as a lion."*

Note what the Bible says, "the coward flees when no one is pursuing." Was that true of Israel? Goliath merely showed his face to the Israelites and on seeing

WHO IS GOLIATH?

him, they began to run away. He and his Philistine army were not even pursuing them. A proverb says "cowards die ten times before their death." Are you like that? You just had a dream of problem, and you packed your things and ran out of town!

> "And all the men of Israel, when they saw the man, fled from him, and were sore afraid." (1Sam. 17:24)

David typifies the righteous being referred to in the scripture; he was as bold as a lion. In fact, this boy was bolder than a lion, he had killed a lion with his bare hands, he sniffed life out of a lion and a bear. His boldness must surpass that of a lion and so too must your boldness if you answer that title 'the righteous.'

> "And David said unto Saul, thy servant kept his father's sheep, and there came a lion, and a bear, and took a lamb out of the flock. And I went out after him and smote him and delivered it out of his mouth and when he arose against me, I caught him by his beard, and smote him." (1Sam. 17:34-35)

David had a track record of boldness and he was not hesitant in declaring it and such record enabled him to see no problem in dealing with Goliath.

WHO IS RIGHTEOUS?

If you surrender your life to Jesus, then His blood redeems you. If you confess your sins, Jesus cleanses you from all unrighteousness. You are made righteous not by your good works or moral rectitude but by the obedience of Jesus in tasting death and shedding His blood for the remission of your sins.

> *"For as by one man's disobedience (i.e. Adam) many were made sinners, so by the obedience of one (i.e. Jesus) shall many be made righteous." (Rom. 5:19)*

Therefore, if you are truly born again, you *must* be righteous and if you are righteous, according to the scripture, you *must* be bold as a lion.

Goliath Killing Prayers boldly declares the word of God, the power of God and the authority of God over all powers, all authorities, all principalities and over whatever is troubling you. You must go forth to your prayer closet and begin to declare that God is greater than your Goliath, no matter how great he may seem in your life.

> *"Let us therefore come boldly unto the throne of grace that we may obtain mercy and find grace to help in time of need." (Heb. 4:16)*

Read that scripture again. How are we supposed to come to God's throne? Not faint-hearted, not cowardly but BOLDLY! God loves the right attitude. The wrong attitude of many is their undoing. The effect of the language of *Hebrew 4:16* is this: If you do not come before God in prayer with an attitude of boldness, you may NOT obtain mercy; you may not find grace to help and you will remain helpless in time of need. Not God's fault. It is entirely your fault, because you refuse to take responsibility and be bold.

PRAYING FOR BOLDNESS

Boldness is an attitude that you cannot hide. It is positive, visible, demonstrative and active. It is extremely important in making prayers purposeful and effective. The early church understood this fact so they set out early in the day to receive boldness. They knew they could not boast of any power of their own; they knew the source of all power is God. They prayed to God for boldness in their prayer lives.

> *"And now Lord behold their threatening and grant unto thy servants that with all boldness they may speak thy word...And when they had prayed, the place was shaken where they were assembled together, and they were all filled with the Holy Ghost and they spake the word of God with boldness." (Acts 4:29, 31)*

They asked for power to speak with boldness and what did they receive immediately? Exactly what they asked for.

> *"Ask and it shall be given you, seek and ye shall find, knock and it shall be opened unto you." (Matt.7:7)*

Paul, the apostle also asked for prayers of boldness on his behalf. In *Ephesians 5:19 20*, we read:

> *"And for me, that utterance may be given unto me that I may open my mouth boldly to make known the mystery of the gospel. For which I am an ambassador in bonds that therein I may speak boldly, as I ought to speak."*

There is a way you ought to speak as a believer; the Bible says that way is to 'SPEAK BOLDLY!'

> *"So that we may boldly say, the Lord is my helper and I will not fear what man shall do unto me." (Heb.13:6)*

I would like you to add, 'I will not fear what Goliath shall do unto me.'

BOLD PEOPLE DO EXPLOITS

With boldness, David did exploits. With boldness, the disciples did exploits, in fact, no Goliath could stand them as they wore the signatory marks of boldness. Miracles happened through bold praying and

and the people acknowledged their boldness. In *Acts 3*, Peter and John prayed boldly for the healing of a lame man and instantly the man was healed. Now the people around them, who saw this incredible miracle, began to wonder how on earth he became healed. What power was in these two unlearned men? But they saw something of note about them. *Acts 4:13* says:

> *"Now when they saw the boldness of Peter and John and perceived that they were unlearned and ignorant men, they marvelled, and they took knowledge of them, that they had been with Jesus."*

What a testimony! If indeed you have been with Jesus, if you are spirit filled and genuinely born again, if you are in a living church where Jesus is being accurately preached, then, people can call you anything they like, but they dare not call you a coward. 'Res ipsa loquitur!' (The boldness in you will speak for itself). Glory to God!

In *Acts 9:27*, we read of how Paul (formerly Saul of Tarsus) "had preached boldly at Damascus in the name of Jesus." Further in verse 29, the Bible says *"he spake boldly in the name of the Lord Jesus, and disputed against the Grecians but they went about to slay him."* You see, boldness can get you into trouble but boldness can also get you out of it. On the other hand, cowardice does not stop trouble from coming, however, such an attitude cannot help you in times of trouble. In *Acts 14:3*, we read of Paul and Barnabas:

> "*Long time therefore abode they speaking boldly in the Lord, which gave testimony unto the word of his grace and granted signs and wonders to be done by their hands.*"

God would always backup those who boldly witness in His Name. Many people are afraid to talk to others about Jesus. Goliath helps them to make all sorts of excuses.

A brother recently shared his testimony with me. One night while he was on a trip abroad, a gang of armed robbers came into his house as he was with his brother. They demanded for all valuables including his international passport, which is considered a valuable 'commodity' in that country. However the brother told them he will not surrender his passport. Incensed at his response, they pulled out their guns and threatened to shoot him. His brother was deadly afraid. This brother then began to declare BOLDLY to the robbers that they could not kill him. He said to them "No weapon fashioned against me will prosper. Your weapon of death cannot prosper against me. I shall not die, but live to declare the glory of the Lord."

The result of this bold declaration was that the gang was not able to shoot him, nor take his passport, and they eventually fled out of the house.

That is what I mean when I say Goliath Killing Prayers are BOLD!

THE HOLY GHOST AND BOLDNESS

The Holy Ghost is the vehicle that transports boldness into the life of a believer. If you are born again, then you must desire to be regularly filled with the Holy Ghost through worship, Word study and praying in tongues.

When the Holy Ghost came upon the disciples in *Acts 2*, they were *instantly transformed*. Peter was a renowned coward who denied Jesus three times, but the baptism of fire (the Holy Ghost) made all the difference. In fact the Holy Ghost anointing was so strong that his first sermon after this experience 'pricked' the hearts of men to the point that they fell on their knees asking for what to do, three thousand of them answered the altar call. His second sermon was equally explosive, five thousand were weeping for their sins and asking Jesus to save them. Thereafter, the ushers lost count! That's Holy Ghost boldness! In *Acts 4:31*, we see boldness closely associated with Holy Ghost baptism.

"And when they had prayed, the place was shaken where they were assembled together, and they were all filled with the Holy Ghost and they spake the word of God with boldness."

To keep your thermometer of boldness always at the increase level, cultivate the habit of praying in tongues. It is the generator of boldness. It is Goliath Killing Prayer.

"But ye, beloved, building up yourselves on your most holy faith, praying in the Holy Ghost." (Jude 20)

"Likewise the spirit also helpeth our infirmities for we know not what we should pray for as we ought but the Spirit itself maketh intercession for us with groanings which cannot be uttered." (Rom.8:26)

PRAYER ARROWS

- *Father I thank you because you make me to reign with Jesus far above all principalities and power and might and dominion and every name that is named (including Goliath) not only in this world but also in that which is to come.*

- *I confess my sins and those of my ancestors. I ask that the blood of Jesus cleanse me from all unrighteousness in the name of Jesus.*

- *I silence every raging of Goliath against my family, my finance and my future in the name of Jesus.*

- *I confess that He that is in me is greater than any Goliath and therefore no weapon of Goliath fashioned against me shall prosper in the name of Jesus.*

- *Lord fill me afresh with your Holy Spirit in the name of Jesus.*

- *Let the spirit of boldness come upon me in the name of Jesus.*

- *I confess now that I have not been given the spirit of fear, but of boldness, of love and of sound mind in the name of Jesus.*

- *Father, empower me to speak the word of God with boldness in the name of Jesus.*

- *Lord, we ask that you embolden all your servants in the mission fields particularly those in the Islamic countries in the name of Jesus.*

- *Lord give me wisdom to know and to remain at my rightful position in Christ Jesus.*

- *I pray for all churches that the undiluted word of God would be preached with boldness in the name of Jesus.*

- *Lord, I come boldly to the throne of grace, let me obtain mercy and find grace to help in time of need in the name of Jesus.*

- *I boldly command every sickness and infirmity in my body to melt away in the name of Jesus.*

- I boldly declare that the season of harvest of souls has come upon our church in the name of Jesus.

- I confess that the Lord is my helper, therefore I shall not fear what Goliath shall do in the name of Jesus.

- Lord, let my life radiate your presence in the name of Jesus.

- Lord give me the tongue of Elijah and let my pronouncements receive heavenly backing in the name of Jesus.

- Holy Spirit, help me to pray as I ought to pray in the name of Jesus.

- Lord, I receive the grace to wax bold in the face of opposition to the gospel in the name of Jesus.

- Father, fill me with boldness to speak the gospel in spite of persecution and contention in the name of Jesus.

- Lord, grant your servants boldness that they may preach the word without fear or respect of persons in the name of Jesus.

Chapter Seven

GKP IS PERSISTENT AND PERSEVERING

"And Eliab, his eldest brother heard when he spake unto the men, and Eliab's anger was kindled against David, and he said, why camest thou hither? And with whom hast thou left those few sheep in the wilderness? I know thy pride, and the naughtiness of thine heart; for thou art come down that thou mightest see the battle. And David said, what have I now done? Is there not a cause?."1Sam.17:28-29

GO BACK TO THE BUSH!

The roadmap to destiny is full of discouragement and disillusionment. However, it is said that history is full of great men and women who overcame discouragement and rose from obscurity to greatness.

I pray you will be one of such great men or women.

David fought against the battle of discouragement

WHO IS GOLIATH?

and disparaging remarks before he could overcome his Goliath. Your own route to greatness may be the same.

The forces of life had taken David from the palace back to the bush where he was tending sheep but divine intervention came when his father sent him to the battle field on an errand serving as a catalyst for his journey and he bagan to make his way back to the palace. The forces of life were waiting for him on the battle field and the one clear goal of these 'forces' was to send him back to the bush. His very own elder brother, Eliab, was a ready willing tool. Is it not written in the words of our Lord Jesus Christ that:

"a man's foes shall be they of his own household." (Matt.10:36)

When his own people were offended at Him, our Lord Jesus Christ said:

"A prophet is not without honour but in his own country and among his own kin, and in his own house." (Mark 6:4)

Eliab was effectively saying to his younger sibling, *"You naughty boy, what are you looking for in the battlefield? You are not trained or meant for this war business; besides, you are a sheep and goat boy. Go back to the bush and do your job there."* (Author's paraphrase)

This was David's first test of discouragement in his journey to fulfil his own destiny. This form of discouragement confronts you with the limitations of where you are coming from and tells you, you cannot get to where you are heading for. But David survived the test through persistence and perseverance. The Bible tells us in *1Sam. 17:30* that David turned away from the source of discouragement.

> *"And he turned from him toward another and spake after the same manner and the people answered him again after the former manner."*

When you are discouraged, learn to turn from the source of discouragement and seek your encouragement elsewhere, most importantly from the Lord.

When this same David went to fight in a battle, the enemies came to his abode of Ziklag, burnt the city down and took captive his wives and children and other followers of his. His own people were even going to stone him, as they were discouraged to almost breaking point. In this uncompromising position he TURNED from them and TURNED to God.

> *"And David was greatly distressed, for the people spake of stoning him, because the soul of all the people was grieved, everyman for his sons and for his daughters: but David encouraged himself in the Lord his God."* (1Sam. 30:6)

The moment David turned to God for encouragement, he was on his way to victory and total recov-

WHO IS GOLIATH?

ery. He persevered in his distress, he persisted in his seeking God and God heard him. God told David,

> "Pursue, for thou shalt surely overtake them, and without fail recover all." (vs8)

David not only recovered all the things he lost to the enemies but he and his army inherited the wealth of their enemies.

> "And David recovered all that the Amalekites had carried away and David rescued his two wives. And there was nothing lacking to them....David recovered all. And David took all the flocks and the herds which they drave before those other cattle and said, this is David's spoil." (vs 18-20)

They were going to keep Blind Bartimeaus a beggar for life. They told him he belonged to the land of the blind and there he was sentenced to remain. However, his persistent and persevering prayer silenced the forces of discouragement as Jesus heard his cry and called for him upon asking what he wanted, Jesus restored his sight.

People can tell you the history of where you are coming from but they don't have the copyright to your future, your future and your destiny is in the hand of God, so turn to Him.

> "But I trusted in thee O Lord, I said, thou art my God. My times are in thy hand, deliver me from the hand of

mine enemies and from them that persecute me."
(Psalm 31:14-15)

YOU ARE WELL ABLE

Another test of discouragement comes in life when we are told that we are not able to do what makes men great. David faced this test. The agent this time was Saul, the king of Israel and when David offered to challenge Goliath, Saul said to him:

"...Thou art not able to go against this Philistine to fight with him for thou art but a youth and he a man of war from his youth." (1Sam.17:33)

For many, that would have been the end of the ambition to kill Goliath. This was a king telling a tiny boy what he could not do so who is the latter to doubt the wisdom of the king. But when the wisdom of the king runs contrary to that of the King of kings, which one do you choose? The Bible says the wisdom of man is foolishness unto God and that God uses the foolish things of this world to confound the wise.

David's response to this challenge was to draw from his past experience with this great God who is able to deliver. He defeated man's wisdom by asserting

WHO IS GOLIATH?

Godly authority and power and recounted how when he was confronted by the ferocious lion and bear that tried to attack a lamb of his flock that, with his own bare hands, he destroyed these wild cannibals. Then came the silencer of discouragement.

"David said moreover, the Lord that delivered me out of the paw of the lion and out of the paw of the bear he will deliver me out of the hand of this Philistine. And Saul said unto David, Go, and the Lord be with thee." (Verse 37)

When you persistently speak the wisdom of God, even in the midst of discouragement, the world has no alternative but to bow to you. The Bible said of Stephen:

"And they were not able to resist the wisdom and the spirit by which he spake." (Acts.6:10)

When the world tells you that you are not able to do great things, tell the world the wisdom of your God, speak the word of God. Let them know you can do *all* things through Christ that strengthens you. Tell them you know your God and hence you shall be strong and do great exploits. Let them know that all things are possible with God whom you serve. Tell them you are well able to do great things and relentlessly persist until your ability becomes reality.

"And Caleb stilled the people before Moses and said Let us go up at once, and possess it for we are well able to

overcome it. But the men that went up with him said, we be not able to go up against the people, for they are stronger than we." (Num.13:31-32)

The men that are going up with you in the journey of life may be discouraged and disenchanted, but you have a duty to be different. You must have another spirit that persists and perseveres for that is the difference between success and failure.

"But my servant Caleb, because he had another spirit with him, and hath followed me fully, him will I bring into the land whereunto he went and his seed shall possess it." (Num. 14:24)

ANOTHER MAN'S SHOES!

A third test of discouragement comes when the world persuades us to do things other peoples' way. They forget that each man is uniquely gifted and differently endowed. It is assumed that what works for A, will automatically work for B. When Saul could not dissuade David from fighting Goliath, he did something else that was equally discouraging.

"And Saul armed David with his armour and he put an helmet of brass upon his head also he armed him with a coat of mail." (1Sam.17:38)

Many people have given up in life due to discouragement. At the root of their discouragement is a long history of trying to fit into other people's shoes, refusing to be what God made them to be, either as a result of ignorance or inaction.

The size of the other man's shoe may be bigger than yours, but do not forget that if you stick to your own size, you are able to cover the same distance if not longer than the other man. Wearing his own shoe size will only delay and diminish you in your journey. This delay and diminishing experience can also discourage and destroy you from reaching your destiny.

David overcame this test by knowing *who he was*, discovering *his own shoes* and insisting on wearing them as he proceeded on the journey to kill Goliath, a journey that would shape his destiny.

> *"And David girded his sword upon his armour and he assayed to go, for he had not proved it. And David said unto Saul, I cannot go with these for I have not proved them. And David put them off him. And he took his staff in his hand and chose him five smooth stones out of the brook, and put them in a shepherd's bag and his sling was in his hand and he drew near to the Philistine." (Vs. 39-40)*

HEALED OF CANCER

The rule of persistence and perseverance in prayer will see you through every test of discouragement and launch you to ultimate victory.

Doctors told a woman she had cancer of the oesophagus. She was given only a few months to live. She went to her Pastor who prayed for her several times but there was no sign of relief. Eventually this woman, on the advice of her Pastor, went to a prayer mountain, where she locked herself in a prayer room, she fasted and prayed for seven days. She had only one prayer point, which she kept saying, and wrote down *"By His stripes I am healed."* She prayed and wrote this prayer point down ten thousand times. On the seventh day, she felt a big relief. She had been totally healed of her ailment. She went to her Pastor radiating in indescribable glory. Her perplexed doctor re-examined her but found no trace of cancer in her. What happened? She refused to give up. She refused to quit. She persisted and persevered in prayer until she prevailed. Wise people say, *'Quitters don't win and winners don't quit!'*

God says we should, *"Pray without ceasing."* Jesus Christ said:

> *"...Men ought always to pray and not to faint"* (Luke18:1)

Discouragement is what makes men to faint. Persistence and perseverance is what makes men to pray always and such men are Goliath Killers. May you be like that in the name of Jesus.

PRAYER ARROWS

- Lord I thank you for setting my feet on the path of full and total recovery.

- Father, give me a clear roadmap to fulfilment of my destiny in the name of Jesus.

- Lord, deliver me from the spirit of abortion and premature termination of destiny in the name of Jesus.

- I receive power over all household enemies in the name of Jesus.

- Father, deliver me from those who persecute me in the name of Jesus.

- Lord, let my persecutors stumble and be ashamed in the name of Jesus.

- I receive power to overcome all forces of discouragement in the name of Jesus.

- I reject the forces of limitations and underachievement in the name of Jesus.

- My destiny would not become an abandoned project in the name of Jesus.

- Holy Spirit, help me to know the mind of God over this particular issue in the name of Jesus (Discuss a particularly bothering issue with the Holy Spirit now).

- *I refuse to yield to the forces of pressures and undue influence in the name of Jesus.*

- *Lord, help me not to sin against you in the name of Jesus.*

- *I receive the grace for persistence in the place of prayer in the name of Jesus.*

- *I receive the grace for perseverance in the place of prayer in the name of Jesus.*

- *I confess that I am well able to overcome Goliath in the name of Jesus.*

- *I receive power to pursue, overtake and recover all in the name of Jesus.*

- *I confess that with God on my side, I will finish the race well and strongly, in the name of Jesus.*

- *Father, let the discouragement of man provoke your encouragement in my life in the name of Jesus.*

- *Lord, strengthen me to pray without ceasing.*

- *Father, answer my prayers and encourage me to pray more in the name of Jesus.*

- *O Lord, reveal unto me the real me in the name of Jesus.*

- *Father, let me know the unique weapons to slay my*

WHO IS GOLIATH?

Goliath and help me to use it in the name of Jesus.

- *I receive the grace for accurate praying and targeted intercession in the name of Jesus.*

- *Thank you Lord for encouraging me in the name of Jesus.*

Chapter Eight

GKP IS POWERFUL AND AUTHORITATIVE

"Then said David to the Philistine, thou comest to me with a sword and with a spear and with a shield but I come to thee in the name of the Lord of Hosts, the God of the armies of Israel, whom thou hast defied." 1Sam.17:45

KEY TO EFFECTIVE PRAYING

Any prayer that lacks power and authority is a useless prayer. You cannot depend on your natural ability to pray successfully, which is why we need the Holy Spirit to help us in prayer.

David knew that part of what frightened Israel was the sheer weight of Goliaths' shield and spear, in fact it took a hefty man to carry his shield. He alone could stop Goliath's weapon from prospering.

"Behold I have created the smith that bloweth the coals in the fire, and that bringeth forth an instrument for his

work and I have created the waster to destroy. No weapon that is formed against thee shall prosper and every tongue that shall rise against thee in judgment thou shalt condemn..." (Isa. 54:16-17)*

Your problem is invoking the power of a demon spirit to fight you. Therefore, you must be able to invoke the power of the Holy Spirit to overcome the problem. Jesus Christ told the disciples:

"You shall receive power after that the Holy Ghost is come upon you..." (Acts 1:8)

They would require this power at all times as they confronted oppositions and problems on the way to fulfilling the Great Commission. We too, because we are born again Christains, filled with the Holy Ghost must operate in similar power today.

POWER IN HIS NAME

The Bible says *"The name of the Lord is a strong tower, the righteous run into it and they are saved." (Pro.18:10)* Those who want to kill Goliath must understand that there is mighty power in the name of the Lord Jesus Christ.

Whilst in the wilderness, Moses fully understood the

authority in the name of the Lord as he invoked it in battles and consistently got victories for Israel over their enemies.

> *"The Lord shall fight for you and ye shall hold your peace." Exo. (14:14)*

When I was coming to sojourn in England some years ago. I knew in my sub-conscious that I was going to battle and took with me a framed picture inscribed with the above scripture. It has served me very well and after seven years still hangs conspicuously in my house. Those powerful words describe my battles and my victories up until today to Gods' glory. Moses also said:

> *"The Lord is a man of war, the Lord is his name." (Exo.15:3)*

Jesus Christ, in His final admonition to the disciples told them:

> *"And whatsoever ye shall ask in my name, that will I do, that the Father may be glorified in the Son. If ye shall ask anything in my name, I will do it." (John 14:14-15)*

That is power and authority that no Goliath or problem can stand. Believers must constantly affirm and boldly confess the name of Jesus in prayer if they want results. The disciples did and they got results.

Goliath Killing Prayers

One day Peter and John were going to the temple to pray when they met at the gate a man lame from his mother's womb. He was a beggar and was looking to them for money. Peter then looked at him and said:

> *"Silver and gold have I none, but such as I have give I thee: In the name of Jesus Christ of Nazareth rise up and walk." (Acts 3:6)*

Instantly the man's feet and anklebone received strength and he leaped up, stood, walked, entered into the temple and began to praise God. Later, when they began to question Peter as to what power and authority healed the man, he said:

> *"And His name through faith in His name hath made this man strong, whom ye see and know: yea, the faith which is by Him hath given him this perfect soundness in the presence of you all." (vs.15)*

Note the phrase in that scripture, *"through faith in His name."* If you don't have faith and belief in the name of Jesus, you better refrain from calling His name. It may backfire. Some people tried that in the Bible. They saw Paul casting out demons in the name of Jesus and as they met a demonic spirit, they too tried to invoke the name of Jesus. But alas! they were unbelievers who neither believed nor had faith in the name and the result was catastrophic for them.

If the world would take everything from you, do not let them take the name of Jesus. It is the power and authority to kill Goliath. That name is exalted above all other names and at the mention of it, every knee, including that of your Goliath, is bound to bow.

> *"Wherefore God also hath highly exalteth and given him a name which is above every name. That at the name of Jesus every knee should bow, of things in heaven, and things in earth, and things under the earth. And that every tongue should confess that Jesus Christ is Lord, to the glory of God the Father." (Phil.2:9-11)*

I have experienced many personal victories in spiritual warfare just by mentioning the name of Jesus. I clearly remember a unique experience, when I was struck by a strange sickness not too long ago. One night in the course of battling with this sickness, I had a dream. In my dream, I was lying on the bed and someone came with a cutlass. This fellow looked evil and ferocious; he raised the cutlass and it was clear he was going to give me a deadly cut. Just as the cutlass was coming down on me, I raised my right arm and shouted the name JESUS! As I screamed His name, the hand that was weilding the cutlass suddenly retreated and could not advance any further. I woke up from the dream and my right arm was actually raised up. 'God-incidentally', the day after this dream also marked the beginning of my recovery from that strange sickness.

"The name of the Lord is a strong tower, the righteous runneth into it and they are safe." (Prov. 18:10)

RELEASE THE POWER

It is sad that God's power and authority lies dormant in many of us. If you believe in the name of Jesus and His words abide in you and He abides in you, then you should be exercising power and authority in His name.

When Jesus gave the disciples power and authority, He expected them to use the power and they did to the glory of God.

"Behold I give unto you power to tread on serpents and scorpions, and over all the power of the enemy and nothing shall by any means hurt you." (Luke 10:19)

These people went to town and put this power into use. The result was tremendous.

"And the seventy returned again with joy saying Lord even the devils are subject unto us through thy name." (vs17)

I pray that every demon will bow to you through the name of Jesus.

Goliath was not a fool and mark you, his father, satan

is not a fool either. When he saw David coming towards him in battle, the Bible says he cursed David by his gods. Goliath has gods, satanically empowered gods. He effectively handed over his battle to his gods. David would have been a big fool if he had no 'god' to hand over his own battle to. That is the problem of those who have no God. The Bible calls them fools.

> *"The fool hath said in his heart, there is no God." (Ps14:1)*

When the devil gets hold of such people, there is no one to deliver them. You cannot afford to stand on the fence. You must choose for yourself whom you want to serve. Joshua said that much to Israel:

> *"And if it seem evil unto you to serve the Lord, choose you this day whom ye will serve; whether the gods which your fathers served that were on the other side of the flood, or the gods of the Amorites in whose land ye dwell: but as for me and my house, we will serve the Lord." (Joshua 24:15)*

When you decide not to follow Jesus, you have decided to follow Baal. There is nothing like indecision!

Problems would come to attack you in the name of their gods. In whose name are you going to confront the problems? Thank God for David, he effectively responded to the curse of Goliath with a counter power, a superpower: *"I come to thee in the name of the*

WHO IS GOLIATH?

Lord of hosts, the God of the armies of Israel..." David said further:

> *"And all this assembly shall know that the Lord saveth not with sword and spear: for the battle is the Lord's and he will give you into our hands." (verse 47)*

God must have been very excited. He felt exalted and glorified. No wonder, he swiftly arose to the occasion and destroyed Goliath. Let God arise and His enemies be scattered.

If we learn to exalt God, proclaim His power and assert His authority, He would feel highly honoured and He would move quickly to our help. David said in one of his Psalms:

> *"The Lord hear thee in the day of trouble; the name of the God of Jacob defend thee; send thee help from the sanctuary and strengthen thee out of Zion; Remember all thy offerings and accept thy burnt sacrifice..." (Ps.20:1-3)*

When we give God the praise, the worship and the honour that is due to Him, He would come down and intervene in our situation. He would confound our Goliaths and send them crashing down.

> *"And when he had consulted with the people, he appointed singers unto the Lord and that should praise the beauty of holiness as they went out before the army, and to say Praise the Lord, for his mercy endureth for*

ever. And when they began to sing and to praise, the Lord set ambushments against the children of Ammon, Moab and Mount Seir, which were come against Judah and they were smitten." (11Chro. 20:21-22)

In the same way your Goliath would be smitten in the name of Jesus.

PRAYER ARROWS

- *Lord I praise the beauty of your holiness. I worship your majesty. I proclaim your dominion, power and authority in the name of Jesus (spend a good time just worshipping Him).*

- *I confess that the name of the Lord is a strong tower, I run into it and I am safe in the name of Jesus.*

- *Lord stretch forth your hand to heal and by the name of your Holy child Jesus, do signs and wonders in this nation.*

- *In the name of the Lord I crush every Goliath under my feet.*

- *In the name of Jesus, no weapon formed against me shall prosper.*

- *I command the knee of every Goliath in my life to bow to the name of Jesus. Lord, be glorified in this land, be glorified in my church and be glorified in my life in the name of Jesus.*

WHO IS GOLIATH?

- I confess that the Lord is on my side, I will not fear, what can man do unto me?

- All nations compass me about, but in the name of the Lord, I will destroy them.

- The enemy compass me as bees, but they are quenched as the fire of thorns, for in the name of the Lord I will destroy them

- Blessed be he that cometh in the name of the Lord. I come against Goliath in the name of the Lord, therefore, I am blessed and victorious.

- Let the Lord thunder from heaven, let the Most High utter His voice in the name of Jesus.

- Lord, make your name known to your adversaries and let the nations tremble at your presence in the name of Jesus.

- Thank you Lord, for your name is great and greatly to be praised.

- In the name of Jesus, let every device of the crafty in my life be disappointed.

- Father, let the hand of the adversary wither in the name of Jesus.

- Lord, your name is Holy, therefore, make me Holy in the name of Jesus.

- Lord, your name is Jehovah Rapha, therefore heal me in the name of Jesus.

- Lord, your name is Jehovah Shalom, therefore, let me experience the peace that is beyond human understanding in the name of Jesus.

- Lord, your name is Jehovah Sabaoth, therefore, take over every battle of my life and fight for me in the name of Jesus.

- Lord, your name is Jehovah Shammah, therefore, I covet your presence all the days of my life in the name of Jesus.

- Lord, your name is Jehovah Mekadishkem, therefore, sanctify me inside out in the name of Jesus.

- Lord, your name is Jehovah Nisi, therefore, cover me with your banner of love in the name of Jesus.

- Let the name of the God of Jacob defend me in the name of Jesus.

- I confess that the Lord is on my side, I will not fear, what can man do unto me?

Chapter Nine

GKP IS FULL OF FAITH

"This day will the Lord deliver thee into mine hand; and I will smite thee, and take thine head from thee; and I will give the carcases of the host of the Philistines this day unto the fowls of the air, and to the wild beasts of the earth; that all the earth may know that there is a God in Israel". 1Sam.17:46

CONSIDER IT DONE

David already had a picture of a dead Goliath. He had not slung a single stone, but he began to proclaim victory over Goliath. No one was left in doubt as to what would happen to Goliath. David had a complete picture. He painted it and displayed it for everyone to see. That is what is called 'Faith'. It is the secret weapon for overcoming your Goliath when you pray. God is full of faith (faithful) and that is what He expects us to be.

WHO IS GOLIATH?

"(As it is written, I have made thee a father of many nations) before him whom he believed even God, who quickeneth the dead, and calleth those things which be not as though they were." (Rom.4:17)

To be effective, your prayer must call those things that be not as if they were. Goliath may still be standing tall before you, but you must not 'see' a standing Goliath, you must see a fallen giant. Faith sees the solution, creates the image or picture of the solution and considers it done. That is what the Bible says in *(Heb.11:1)*

"NOW FAITH is the substance of things hoped for, the evidence of things not seen."

'Now Faith' brings the future to the present, declares the future to be present and this is necessary to please God.

"But without faith it is impossible to please him, for he that cometh to God must believe that he is, and that he is a rewarder of them that diligently seek him." (Heb.11:6)

Many times, God enjoins us to live by faith: *"The just shall live by his faith"* (Hab.2:4); *"The just shall live by faith"* (Rom.1:17; Gal.3:11; Heb.10:38)

Whatever you want God to do for you, when you pray, you must consider it done before you can see it done. Jesus taught that principle in *(Mark 11:22-24)*

"And Jesus answering saith unto them, Have faith in God. For verily I say unto you that whosoever shall say unto this mountain, be thou removed and be thou cast into the sea and shall not doubt in his heart but shall believe that those things which he saith shall come to pass he shall have whatsoever he saith. Therefore I say unto you what things soever ye desire, when ye pray, believe that ye receive them, and ye shall have them."

From the above words of Jesus, let me give you the following points in relation to overcoming your Goliath:

> Have faith in God that you are able to overcome Goliath.

> Say (i.e. vocalise) to your Goliath exactly what you want to befall him. Get a clear picture or image of your desire.

> Do not entertain any doubt in your mind. Your words must be strong, powerful and assertive.

> Believe unequivocally that what you vocalise would happen.

> Feed your confessions with commensurate actions.

> Wait for the manifestation.

If you return to *1Sam.17: 46,* you will see again David's Goliath Killing Prayer. All the six points enumerated above were present and every one of David's desires came to pass. **Likewise, may every one of your desires in prayer this year come to pass in the name of Jesus.**

HEALING IS BY FAITH.

If it is impossible to please God without faith, I submit that it is impossible to get divinely healed without some measure of faith. The Bible says in *James 5:15 "And the prayer of faith shall save the sick..."* Conversely, it can be said that the prayer without faith shall not save the sick. The prayer of faith is a prayer by a person who has a firm and doubtless conviction that God will indeed heal him or the person prayed for.

When we study healing in the ministry of our Lord Jesus Christ, we would see the idea of faith echoing all through the healing processes.

On the faith of the centurion who prayed Jesus for the healing of his sick servant, Jesus said: *"Verily I say unto you, I have not found so great faith, no, not in Israel"* (Matt.8:10). Of the woman with the twelve years of affliction, Jesus commented on her faith for healing thus: *"Daughter, be of good comfort; thy faith hath made thee whole." (Matt.9:22).* When two blind men came praying to Jesus that He should heal them, He touched their eyes and said, *"According to your faith be it unto you." (Matt.9:29).* A Canaanite whose daughter was demon possessed came to Jesus begging for healing. She was ignored and disparaged by Jesus, but she maintained her faith, conviction and persistence. The Master had this to say about her 'faith-attitude': *"O woman, great is thy faith, be it unto thee even as thou wilt." (Matt. 15:28).* There was hardly any healing miracle Jesus performed that did not draw comments about the faith of the patients.

If you lack faith for your healing, ask God to give you today. The disciples of Jesus once asked Him to increase their faith *(Luke 17:5)*. Receive faith through the word of God, hearing it, believing it, confessing it and acting it. *"...Faith cometh by hearing and hearing by the word of God." (Rom.10: 17).*

The same way David painted an image of a dead Goliath with his head caught off, and confessed this with his mouth is the way you are to paint an image of your healthy self and confess aloud that you have already been healed. When you continue in this confession with scriptural power and authority, the words of God become spirit and life releasing healing into your body.

"It is the spirit that quickeneth; the flesh profiteth nothing: the words that I speak unto you, they are spirit, and they are life." (John 6:63)

FAITH TESTIMONIES

Some years ago, the doctors said my wife had a big fibroid. They also said that was one of the reasons she could not successfully get pregnant. We began to pray about it to God for divine healing. She was then referred to another hospital for further diagnosis and preparation for an operation. While she was waiting to be attended to, she spent the time to praise and thank God for her divine healing. She continued this praise warfare for about one hour. The doctors eventually called her in. They used every sophisticated gadget to locate the fibroid but they could not find it again. In their disbelief, they called other experts in. They too could not find the fibroid. My wife's faith had made her whole at that hour. Praise God!

There is also this moving testimony of faith from a sister in our church. She heard a sermon that encouraged her to apply faith to her condition. She was trusting God for a husband. She bought a little notepad and wrote at the opening page of the notepad the scripture **Romans 4:17** *"..God…who…calleth those* *things which be not as though they were."* She then began to write love letters to her 'husband'. She did this everyday on this notepad, telling this unseen 'husband' everything happening to her and how much she longed to meet him and be his wife. This faith exercise continued for one month or so. She had prayed to God that her husband should manifest before she finished up the notepad.

Miraculously, two pages to the end of the notepad, she received an e-mail from a man who lived six thousand miles away from her. This man said God had told him that she is his wife! She burst into tears. She showed me this notepad, which I kept for one week, I could not but shed tears as I read this faith saturated 'letters'. Indeed, a case of calling those things which be not as though they were. You too can move in the same dimension of faith, if you believe.

> *"NOW FAITH is the substance of things hoped for, the evidence of things not seen." (Heb. 11:1)*

As I am writing this chapter, I see the people of Iraq on the television dragging the statues of their 'President', Saddam Hussein around the streets of Baghdad. They are crushing and cursing his image. I am saying to myself: They have pronounced a death sentence on this man. This act of faith alone marks his exit from power and could even mark the

WHO IS GOLIATH?

end of his life on earth. The people have created the 'substance of things hoped for' (the collapse of Saddam's regime) and the 'evidence of things not seen' (the funeral of Saddam Hussein).

It is time to do the same for your Goliath!

PRAYER ARROWS

- *Lord I praise you, for you are faithful and you keep covenant and mercy with them that love you.*

- *Lord, I repent from the destructive sin of doubt and unbelief in the name of Jesus.*

- *I command every anti-miracle agent to depart from my life in the name of Jesus.*

- *Today, I receive deliverance from the spirit of doubt and I vacate the wilderness of unbelief in the name of Jesus.*

- *Lord, increase my faith in the name of Jesus.*

- *By faith I crush my Goliath and I cut off his head in the name of Jesus.*

- *By faith I cross my red sea and I walk on dry ground in the name of Jesus.*

- *By faith, I command every wall of Jericho confronting me to fall flat in the name of Jesus.*

- Lord, let your servants be full of faith and the Holy Spirit in the name of Jesus.

- I receive the grace to live by faith in the name of Jesus.

- I receive the grace to walk by faith and not by sight in the name of Jesus.

- By faith, I receive divine healing in every area of my life in the name of Jesus.

Chapter Ten

GKP IS PRE-EMPTIVE AND OFFENSIVE

"And it came to pass when the Philistine arose and came and drew near to meet David, that David hasted and ran toward the army to meet the Philistine." 1Sam.17:48

There is a saying that the best form of defence is attack. I see that happen in physical warfare. We need to see it happen in spiritual warfare, which is the mother of all warfare.

A Goliath Killing Prayer is pre-emptive. It is offensive not defensive. The rule is: Do not wait for the problem to strike, strike at the problem before it strikes at you. Let us examine how David used this strategy to kill Goliath.

WHO IS GOLIATH?
STEPS TO OFFENSIVE PRAYERS

> *"And it came to pass when the Philistine arose, and came and drew nigh to meet David, that David hasted and ran toward the army to meet the Philistine. And David put his hand in his bag, and took thence a stone and slang it, and smote the Philistine in his forehead that the stone sunk into his forehead and he fell upon his face to the earth." (1Sam. 17:48-49)*

David took three pre-emptive steps to defeat Goliath. First, the bible says he hasted. Second, he ran to meet the adversary. Third, he fired the first salvo. I watched the coalition forces employing this strategy against Iraq. The forces hasted against the enemy at every turn. They ran to meet the enemies wherever they could be found and they carried out so much bombardment against the enemy locations such that the latter was left confused and disoriented in most cases.

God expects us to do the same in spiritual warfare. Pray aggressively against a problem before it strikes at you. Let us confirm this through scriptures.

OFFENSIVE PRAYERS ARE FORCEFUL

> *"From the days of John the Baptist until now, the kingdom of heaven has been forcefully advancing and force-*

ful men lay hold of it." (Matt.11:12 N.I.V)

The expression *'forceful men lay hold of it'* does not sound defensive. It sounds more like a man who hasted, ran and fired the first salvo like David. The Amplified version of the Bible says *"...violent men seize it by force (as a precious prize – a share in the heavenly kingdom is sought with most ardent zeal and intense exertion)."* Anyone trying to seize something by force always strikes first.

Jesus Christ also said in *Matt. 12:29 "Or else how can one enter into a strong man's house and spoil his goods, except he first bind the strongman? And then he will spoil his house."* Note the word 'first' in this saying. You must be the first to strike in prayer. In similar vein we read in *Luke 11:21-22 "When a strong man armed keepeth his palace, his goods are in peace: but when a stronger than he shall come upon him, and overcome him, he taketh from him all his armour wherein he trusted and divideth his spoils."*

If you have Jesus in your life, you are stronger than any problem. So what do you do? *"Come upon"* that problem in prayer, *"overcome"* that problem and *"take from him all his armour wherein he trusted."*

An African proverb says if someone is approaching you with a long stick, you do not allow the person to get so close before you launch a protest. Your protest must be launched while the danger is still far away.

Do not wait for sickness to strike at you before you start praying for divine health. Do not wait until your wedding day before you attack marriage destroyers. Do not wait until that bad dream manifests itself in the physical before you battle to cancel it. The word of God is on your side as a sure offensive weapon.

OFFENSIVE PRAYERS ARE PROPHETIC.

"Thus saith the Lord God, it shall not stand, neither shall it come to pass." (Isaiah. 7:7)

"That thou shall take up this proverb against the king of Babylon and say: How hath the oppressor ceased! The golden city ceased! The Lord hath broken the staff of the wicked, and the sceptre of the rulers. He who smote the people in wrath with a continual stroke, he that ruled the nations in anger is persecuted and none hindereth" Isa. (14:4-5)

Take a look at the above scripture again and check what happened recently in Iraq, the modern day Babylon. See how the oppressor has ceased. Look at what happened to the golden palaces. A mockery of their old glamour. They now lie desolate, desecrated and decimated.

ETERNAL VIGILANCE

It is said that eternal vigilance is the price of liberty. Those who want to be free from the oppression of Goliath must be vigilant. Those who desire to take hold of the victory of the cross and enjoy the freedom of that victory must not be unaware of the devices of the enemy. They must be steadfast and immovable. They must pray in and out of season without ceasing and without giving up.

About two years ago, a couple came to me. They have been married for four years and have been trying for a child without success. They have tried some expensive medical helps, which did not succeed. They were just about to try another. We prayed and I asked if they could put a hold on another expensive treatment and let us seek the face of God for a while.

Upon further spiritual mapping of their situation, the wife explained that she had been having some terrible dreams lately. Those dreams were directly related to her reproduction. We began to pray offensively against those dreams, forbidding them from standing or coming to pass. After a while, the dreams just disappeared. Then a few months after, the lady conceived. Now, God has blessed the couple with a beautiful baby girl.

"Be well balanced...be vigilant and cautious at all times for that enemy of yours, the devil roams around like a lion roaring...seeking someone to seize upon and devour. Withstand him; be firm in faith (against his onset - rooted, established, strong, immovable, and determined)..." (1Pet.5:8) (Amplified).

PRAYER ARROWS

▶ *Father, I thank you because your eyes travel to and fro the whole earth watching on my behalf.*

▶ *Lord make me an offensive weapon of war and a formidable battle axe in the name of Jesus.*

▶ *Lord, baptise me with the Jehu anointing of zeal and righteousness in the name of Jesus.*

▶ *Lord be my Rock of offence against the adversary in the name of Jesus.*

▶ *I forbid every evil counsel concerning me from coming to pass in the name of Jesus.*

▶ *I cancel every satanic dream and I forbid it from coming to pass in the name of Jesus.*

- *Let every wicked counsel be turned to foolishness in the name of Jesus.*

- *I command all demonic network to break in the name of Jesus.*

- *Let evil foundations be uprooted and destroyed in the name of Jesus.*

- *Let every power hiding under the cover of darkness to do evil be destroyed in the name of Jesus.*

- *I command the wind, the waters, the earth and the air to refuse to co-operate with my adversaries.*

- *Let every adversary of open doors in my life be scattered in the name of Jesus.*

- *Let God arise and His enemies be scattered in the name of Jesus.*

- *I prophesy that my tomorrow would be alright in the name of Jesus.*

Chapter Eleven

GKP IS PREVAILING

"So David prevailed over the Philistine with a sling and with a stone, and smote the Philistine and slew him; but there was no sword in the hand of David. Therefore David ran, and stood upon the Philistine, and took his sword and drew it out of the sheath thereof and slew him and cut off his head therewith. And when the Philistines saw their champion was dead, they fled."
1Sam. 17:50-51

The story says that after David had struck Goliath with a stone from his sling, the latter *'fell upon his face to the earth' (verse 49)*. However, David did not turn back and say the battle was over. It is not over until you have won. He remained vigilant. He still ran, took the sword of the enemy and cut off his head. In addition to Goliath falling in the previous verse, something else happened at this stage. The followers of Goliath fled now that they saw that their champion was dead.

The job was only half done with the falling of Goliath. His followers were still waiting and watching. However when David cut off the head of Goliath, nobody could take over from him. They all fled. That is what prevailing prayers do. All those waiting to perpetuate your problem would flee once they see that you have prevailed in prayer.

PREVAILING PRAYER IS GOAL FOCUSED

When we pray, there must be a goal and we must be focused on that goal and keep praying until the goal is achieved. Jacob did that. His goal was to be blessed by the Lord. He kept wrestling with the angel and refused to let him go until he had achieved that goal. That is prevailing prayer.

> *"And Jacob was alone and there wrestled a man with him until the breaking of the day. And when he saw that he prevailed not against him, he touched the hollow of his thigh and the hollow of Jacob's thigh was out of joint as he wrestled with him. And he said Let me go for the day breaketh. And he said, I will not let thee go except thou bless me. And he said unto him, what is thy*

name? And he said, Jacob. And he said, thy name shall be called no more Jacob, but Israel, for as a prince has thou power with God and with men and hast prevailed...And he blessed him there." (Gen 32:24-29)

In the warfare described above, both parties were fighting to prevail. We read the word 'prevail' twice in those verses. Eventually, Jacob prevailed. When you prevail in spiritual warfare, you will prevail in physical warfare.

TO PREVAIL, YOU MUST TRAVAIL

In order to prevail in prayer, you must be ready to travail. That is not a simple term. When a woman labours at childbirth, she is travailing and some prayers, to become effective must be agonising.

John Knox prayed in agony when he cried: *"Lord, give me Scotland or I die."* He prevailed because Queen Mary of Scotland later said, *"I fear the prayer of John Knox more than the whole French army put together."* Jesus travailed in agonising prayer at Gethsemane against the powers of darkness until He prevailed.

> *"And being in an agony he prayed more earnestly: and his sweat was as it were great drops of blood falling*

down to the ground." (Luke 22:44)

God saw His travail coming and spoke of it more than six hundred years before the Gethsemane experience through the lips of prophet Isaiah:

> *"He shall see of the travail of his soul, and shall be satisfied: by his knowledge shall my righteous servant justify many; for he shall bear their iniquities." (Isa.53: 11)*

Paul also understood the need to travail if he must prevail in intercession. He said concerning the brethren at the Galatians' church:

> *"My little children of whom I travail in birth again until Christ be formed in you." (Gal. 4:19)*

Much prayer needs have become abandoned projects because those praying are either too lazy or too hasty to travail until they prevailed. God wants the church to travail in prayers if she would witness a spiritual rebirth and renewal called revival.

> *"A voice of noise from the city, a voice from the temple, a voice of the Lord that rendereth recompense to his enemies…for as soon as Zion travailed, she brought forth her children." (Isa. 66:6,8)*

If we want to hear the voice of God confirming our victory, we must raise a voice through citywide prayer campaign and also a voice through the agonising intercessions of the church.

PREVAILING PRAYER IS PASSIONATE

Many Christians are praying without passion, hence they lack the capacity to prevail or effectively hit the target. Passion is that desperate urge to get desired result. We see it in Hannah. She prevailed because she prayed with passion. Her total being was involved in the praying. Everything within her vibrated and cried unto God for divine intervention. Even the priest in the church where she prayed was baffled by her passionate plea in prayer to God.

> "And she was in bitterness of soul, and prayed unto the Lord, and wept sore...And it came to pass as she continued praying before the Lord, that Eli marked her mouth. Now Hannah, she spake in her heart only her lips moved, but her voice was not heard: therefore Eli thought she had been drunken... and Hannah answered...I am a woman of a sorrowful spirit...have poured out my soul before the Lord...out of the abundance of my complaint and grief have I spoken hitherto." (1Sam.1:10-16)

Heaven had no choice but to respond to the passionate cry of that woman. She prevailed and brought forth a miracle child. **May you prevail and bring forth the miracle you have been travailing for in prayer in the name of Jesus.**

In *Gen.30:1*, Rachel prayed passionately. Although her prayer was misdirected, God took notice and answered her. In *verse 22*, it is written,

> "And God remembered Rachel, and God hearkened to her, and opened her womb"

Rachel herself was to say later in Gen.30:8

> "And Rachel said, with great wrestling's have I wrestled with my sister, and I have prevailed and she called his name Napthali."

What Rachel did not understand was that her wrestling was not physical but spiritual.

> "For we wrestle not against flesh and blood, but against principalities, against powers, against rulers of the darkness of this world, against spiritual wickedness in high places." (Eph.6:12)

Today, ask yourself, How desperate am I for an answer to prayers? Turn your desperation into passionate praying. God will surely remember you and you will prevail in the name of Jesus.

As you leave this chapter, remember the following Rules of War:

1. Don't leave the enemy half dead

2. Don't leave the problem half solved

3. Pray until you pray through

4. Pray until something happens

5. Pray until you prevail

PRAYER ARROWS

➤ *Father, I thank you because Jesus Christ prevailed on the cross and gave me victory.*

➤ *Lord, empower me to prevail over my Goliath in the name of Jesus.*

➤ *Lord, deliver me from the spirit of abandoned projects in the name of Jesus.*

➤ *Every good thing the Lord has started in my life would be completed to His glory in the name of Jesus.*

➤ *I refuse to yield to the spirit of failure at the edge of success in the name of Jesus.*

➤ *Lord open my eyes and let me locate solution in every problem in the name of Jesus.*

➤ *Lord, give me a soul thirst for prevailing prayers in the name of Jesus.*

➤ *Lord, hear the passionate prayer of every 'Hannah', remember them and let them bring forth their miracles in the name of Jesus.*

WHO IS GOLIATH?

- *Let the dying fire upon my altar be rekindled in the name of Jesus.*

- *I forbid frustration from quenching the fire upon my altar in the name of Jesus.*

- *I forbid discouragement from quenching the fire upon my altar in the name of Jesus.*

- *Let every power prolonging my problem be disgraced permanently in the name of Jesus.*

- *I refuse to die unfulfilled in the name of Jesus.*

- *O Lord, let not man prevail over me in the name of Jesus.*

- *I shall prevail over every evil tongue raised against me in the name of Jesus.*

- *The gates of hell shall not prevail against the church in the name of Jesus.*

- *Let the sword of the enemy return to him, let him fall on his own sword in the name of Jesus.*

- *Father, give me the passion of Elijah to prevail in prayer in the name of Jesus.*

Chapter Twelve

WHOSE SON ART THOU?

"And Saul said to him, whose son art thou, thou young man? And David answered, I am the son of thy servant Jesse, the Bethlehemite." 1Sam.17:58

When David began to charge against Goliath, everyone was amazed, including Saul, the king of Israel. Saul asked one of his commanders, Abner, *"Whose son is this youth?"* Abner could not tell, because, this youth was taking an extraordinary step. He was running toward what every one else was running away from: Goliath. It takes a giant killer to kill a giant killer.

There is a deeper meaning to the query Saul raised about David. It simply means that not everybody can confront Goliath and overcome him. They must be peculiar people of peculiar breed.

"But ye are a chosen generation a royal priesthood, an

WHO IS GOLIATH?

holy nation, a peculiar people that ye should show forth the praises of him who hath called you out of darkness into his marvellous light." (1Pet.2:9)

People who cannot correctly answer the question: *"Whose son art thou?"* must not venture against demons and Goliath was carrying many demons. If you are not the son or daughter of the 'right person', you may never get away with certain things. We saw an interesting story in *Acts chapter 19* of a similar question being raised.

"Then certain of the vagabond Jews, exorcists, took upon them to call over them which had evil spirits the name of the Lord Jesus, saying we adjure you by Jesus whom Paul preacheth. And there were seven sons of one Sceva, a Jew, and chief of the priests, which did so. And the evil spirit answered and said Jesus I know and Paul I know but who are ye? And the man in whom the evil spirit was leaped on them, and overcame them and prevailed against them, so that they fled out of that house naked and wounded." (verses 13-16)

They suffered for doing what Jesus and Paul did and got away with. Reason: they were the sons of the wrong person.

When Saul asked David whose son he was, David replied: *"I am the son of thy servant Jesse the Bethlehemite."* David must have drunk from the same source as Jesus: The Rivers of God. *Isaiah 11:10* speaks of Jesus:

> *"And in that day there shall be a root of Jesse, which shall stand for an ensign of the people; to it shall the Gentiles seek: and his rest shall be glorious."*

We also read of this wonderful 'family tree' in *Rev.5:5*

> *"And one of the elders saith unto me, Weep not: behold the Lion of the tribe of Judah, the Root of David hath prevailed to open the book and to loose the seven seals thereof."*

Jesus Christ says of Himself in *Rev.(22:16:)*

> *"I Jesus have sent mine angel to testify unto you these things in the churches. I am the root and the offspring of David and the bright and morning star."*

Following Paul's encounter with Jesus and having fully surrendered, his identity changed. He had become the son of a Father at the mention of whose name Goliath must bow. Of this relationship, Paul said:

> *"For as many as are led by the Spirit of God, they are the sons of God. For ye have not received the spirit of bondage again to fear; but ye have received the Spirit of adoption, whereby we cry, Abba Father. The Spirit itself beareth witness with our spirit that we are the children of God." (Rom.8:15-16)*

WHO IS GOLIATH?

You are either a child of God or a child of the devil. There is no middle course. A child of God is the one who has surrendered his/her life to Jesus. They are the people who can answer the question *"Whose son art thou?"* correctly. Goliath would bow at their feet and demons would tremble at their approach. They are no ordinary people, they are peculiar, and they are new creatures.

> *"Therefore, if any man be in Christ, he is a new creature: old things are passed away, behold all things are become new." (2Cor.5:17)*

If you have not given your life to Jesus, or you are in any doubt about your salvation, I want to invite you to come to Jesus right now and let Him transform and renew you. Let Him give you a new name. Jesus says in *(Rev.2:17)*

> *"He that hath an ear, let him hear what the Spirit saith unto the churches. To him that overcometh will I give…a new name written which no man knoweth saving he that receiveth it."*

If that sounds like you, I have no doubt that you are ready to overcome and be victorious over every Goliath in your life. Therefore join me straightaway in praying the following prayer aloud:

> *Father, I, (mention your name aloud) come to you today in the name of Your dear Son Jesus Christ. I confess my sins and forsake them. I repent from my transgressions*

and those of my ancestors. I confess that Jesus Christ came for the very purpose of destroying the works of sins in my life. He shed His precious blood on the cross for the remission of my sins. Today, I acknowledge Jesus as my Lord and Saviour. Therefore, Lord Jesus, have mercy on me, give me a new name and write that name in the book of life. I will worship you, I will serve you and by your grace I will not backslide in the name of Jesus. Thank you Lord for saving me and giving me victory over Goliath now and forever. Amen.

Congratulations! You have killed your Goliath. Now move to the palace and reign forever with Jesus Christ, the King of kings and the Lord of lords! You are not going back to 'Shepherdbush' again, you are in the palace to stay and to reign!

"And Saul took him that day, and would let him go no more home to his father's house." (1Sam.18:2)

I love this song of victory that someone taught me:

"Yesterday I killed the Lion

Today, I slay Goliath

And tomorrow
I can do all things

Through Christ that strengthens me."

WHO IS GOLIATH?

I want to hear from you. Please send your comments about this book to me in care of the address below. Thank you.

RCCG VICTORY HOUSE

5 Congreve Street, Old Kent Road

London. SE17 1TJ

E-mail: Leke@Sanusi.fsnet.co.uk,

Tel.: 020 7252 7522